LEARNING-TO-TEACH
CASES AND CONCEPTS FOR NOVICE TEACHERS AND TEACHER EDUCATORS

Carol A. Beynon
Arthur N. Geddis
Barry A. Onslow
University of Western Ontario

Prentice
Hall

Toronto

Canadian Cataloguing in Publication Data

Beynon, Carol, 1950–
    Learning-to-teach: cases and concepts for novice teachers and teacher educators

Includes bibliographical references and index.
ISBN 0-13-16655-3

1. Teaching. 2. Teachers – Training of. I. Geddis, Arthur N. (Arthur Norman), 1941– . II. Onslow, Barry A. III. Title.

LB1025.3.B49 2001   371.102   C00-930955-1

0-13-016655-3

Vice President, Editorial Director: Michael Young
Senior Acquisitions Editor: Kathleen McGill
Senior Marketing Manager: Christine Cozens
Developmental Editor: Tammy Scherer
Production Editor: Sherry Torchinsky
Copy Editor: Krysia Lear
Production Coordinator: Peggy Brown
Page Layout: Carol Magee
Art Director: Mary Opper
Cover Design: Sarah Battersby
Cover Image: PhotoDisc

1 2 3 4 5   05 04 03 02 01

Printed and bound in Canada

CONTENTS

Preface

INTRODUCTION

This book is written to engage teachers, both novice and experienced, in the process of *learning-to-teach* through the acquisition of knowledge and the development of discussion and reflective practice. The book has been designed to assist student teachers, cooperating teachers, and faculty advisors as part of a community of learners in expanding the understanding of learning-to-teach. Each chapter focuses on teacher development at the preservice and university level, and is especially relevant for those educators focusing on field experiences and the practicum.

Learning-to-teach is a complex and ongoing process, and novice teachers find themselves in a professional setting that seems patterned, yet somewhat ambiguous and peremptory. Complicating the process of developing a scholarship of learning-to-teach is the familiarity that everyone in society has with what teachers do because they have observed it first-hand as pupils. The basic means of educating teachers is similar across the English-speaking world: student teachers study teaching and pedagogy with university-based teacher educators, and then practise their teaching in schools with experienced teacher educators, known universally as cooperating teachers. Even though a remarkable similarity exists in the patterns of educating teachers across North America, we have no agreement on how to prepare the best teachers, nor do we understand fully how students learn to teach.

Much has been written about the kind of academic background and personal qualities needed to become a good teacher. Other reports have described the negative features of current teacher education programs. All reports allege serious problems with preservice teacher education programs and many point to student teaching as problematic. None, however, investigate in any depth the roles of students, cooperating teachers, and university-based teacher educators in learning-to-teach, or how experiences in the practicum significantly influence student teachers' practices as beginning teachers. This book fills a gap that exists in preservice teacher education literature. It provides a useful academic protocol for educators to learn about their roles in helping students to become teachers.

We believe university faculty must work collaboratively with cooperating teachers in professional development programs that bring teacher educators together within a community of learners. Indeed, much of this book grew out of a year-long course for cooperating teachers that we have co-developed and taught at the University of Western Ontario for the past eight years.

Much is known about the influential role of cooperating teachers in shaping the practices of novice teachers. Little research, however, focuses on how cooperating teachers help or prevent beginning teachers from becoming competent agents of change and consequently making improvements in the school system. Our last chapter explores some possibilities for shaping agents of change.

This text will encourage its readers to:

* be open-minded and stretch their belief systems;
* be willing to share perspectives and beliefs with others;
* listen carefully to and respect the thoughts and values of others; and
* recognize that *all* teachers control the extent and pace of their own professional learning.

FEATURES

The primary purpose of this book is to focus attention on the roles of the student teacher, the cooperating teacher, and the university-based teacher educator in learning-to-teach. As well, the book provides a collection of authentic cases and questions that can be used during discussions about teaching. It is designed to build a *community of professional practice* for all levels of educators. This book is also intended to assist all teachers in verbalizing a *pedagogy of scholarship* that helps educators articulate and examine tacit and explicit practices of teaching.

With the exception of the first and final chapters, each chapter is written in two parts. In the first part, we discuss the topic using a conceptual framework to articulate, frame, and reframe the issue, drawing on relevant literature and insights about teacher education. The second part features original case studies that illustrate the topic or issue, then concludes with a series of questions to promote discussion, generate some cognitive dissonance, and further learning.

This book employs cases collected by the authors during student teaching sessions. Each case is based on a real situation and has been researched and co-written with student teachers, cooperating teachers, and university professors. Some of the cases have been written from only one perspective, while others have been written from the perspective of a second person in the same situation. In such cases, the stories turn out to be quite different as the reader examines the case from the different perspectives of the participants. This re-framing leads to a deeper understanding of the issues and complexities facing teacher education, especially during field experiences.

Case studies have been chosen because they provide a *real-life* documentary of practice for student teachers and provide multiple opportunities for discussion about significant issues faced. These cases are written to facilitate opportunities for teacher educators to discuss pre-service teacher education in the context of lived experience; the emotional involvement of the participants is portrayed in the context of actual classrooms. While the cases have been chosen to focus class discussions on particular aspects of the supervision process, numerous other issues permeate the material, just as happens in the complicated setting of real classrooms. In order to work through the cases, participants will have to deal with both primary and superficial issues. Further, we did not write the cases as typical examples of practice, rather, we constructed them to be typical of the problematic situations practicum participants experienced. The cases invite readers to engage in discussions of the various problems, to examine and consider alternative solutions, and to reflect on personal practices.

Readers of the preliminary drafts of this book have indicated that they have found it informative and insightful because the information relates directly to their work as teachers. The following comments are representative of their feedback:

> Questions that came out of discussion of the cases stay with you and so you are always thinking and inquiring into your behaviour not only as a classroom teacher but as a teacher educator (A cooperating teacher).

The affirmation of the importance of clear, honest and open communication has made me reconsider my own practice (A cooperating teacher).

I have truly valued these opportunities for discussion so much because they inform my own practice and pedagogical content knowledge in terms of my own university classroom (A university-based teacher educator).

Our readers have indicated that the book provides student teachers and teacher educators with opportunities to think critically about their roles, practices, and influence in learning-to-teach and how they can be improved, as well as creating open dialogue about teacher practices, thinking, and actions in teacher education.

ORGANIZATION

This text is divided into four sections. The introductory section provides the foundation for the book through an in-depth exploration of the current context of preservice teacher education. We begin in Chapters 1 and 2 by describing the background of preservice teacher education as it is currently understood in North American universities and schools. We also examine critically the place of the practicum experience in teacher education. In Chapter 1, we ask the readers to ground and frame their own experiences in learning-to-teach by completing a critical incident activity. The first case studies complete Chapter 2.

In section 2, we lay out a conceptual framework for learning-to-teach based on effective problem-solving, and provide strategies for student teachers and teacher educators to use when faced with managing difficult issues. In Chapter 3, we discuss reflection in thinking and action, and provide examples of how reflection-in-action and reflection-on-action (Schön, 1987) can facilitate discussions about teaching and learning. In Chapter 4, we discuss the inevitability of the problematic situations that occur during student teaching, and offer examples as to how teacher educators manage, rather than resolve, the dilemmas. The politics of teaching, including the often taboo subjects of power and authority in professional education, is the focus of Chapter 5. We complete this section with two important chapters about the roles of teachers and communication skills.

In section 3, we examine many of the major issues in preservice teacher education (including gender, race and class issues; inclusive classrooms; classroom management; and student teacher evaluation) that surface through problematic case studies. These chapters, through the conceptual framework and ensuing case studies, provide context and opportunity for teacher educators and their student teachers to reflectively explore strategies that might be employed in difficult situations.

In the concluding chapter, we explore a professional future for teacher education, and consider the option of helping novice teachers to become agents of change as they enter the school system as professionals. We address the responsibilities of both school-based and university-based teacher educators to help empower new teachers in becoming *agents of change* in a traditional and conservative school system. We discuss how this focus can better occur in a collaborative environment, where teacher educators work together in a community of professional practice to develop preservice teacher education programs that emanate from reflective-based practice.

The book is based on the current knowledge of teaching, and makes an important contribution to teacher education in that it furthers the professional knowledge base of teaching for both experienced and beginning teachers. We have sought to:

- bring student teachers, cooperating teachers, and university practitioners together in a community of professional practice, providing a conceptual framework and series of case studies that illuminate and further the professional knowledge base of learning-to-teach;

- examine the role of the student teaching experience in relation to the university-based component of preservice teacher education;

- examine the roles of each of the major participants in the practicum triad;

- examine the school as a suitable site for teacher education, with a primary emphasis on investigating and articulating the role of the cooperating teacher; and

- encourage the development of reflective problem-solving among teacher educators.

While the concepts of learning-to-teach that we develop in the book are complex, we have attempted to retain their sense and integrity while making the writing accessible. With the use of the numerous case studies, the book has many examples from which students of education, whether novice or experienced teacher, can learn in any venue. The questions at the end of each chapter highlight key points and aim to stimulate informed discussions and decision-making.

SUPPLEMENTS

An Instructors' Manual is available which provides an overview of how to connect theory and practice by teaching with case studies. Each chapter guide includes a summary, definitions of central concepts, and either suggested supplementary activities or a discussion of the case study and accompanying questions.

ACKNOWLEDGEMENTS

We wish to acknowledge the support and assistance of numerous people in the writing of this book, namely our University of Western Ontario graduate assistants, Linda Hawkins and Susan Ackland, for their research and preliminary crafting of several of the case studies, and Rachel Hayden and Igor Sukonnik for their editorial assistance.

We thank the cooperating teachers who were co-learners with us over the past eight years and who helped build a community of scholars. In particular we would like to thank Wendy Crocker of the Thames Valley District School Board, teacher and teacher educator, who was a co-learner and instructor with us for several of the courses with our cooperating teachers.

Thanks also to the student and novice teachers who often taught us more than we taught them, and who shared their stories and insights with us for the case studies; and to our colleague Colin Laine for his insightful comments and suggestions on the inclusive education chapter.

We also thank the many faculty members who have assisted us in questioning our practice and refining our thoughts, especially these reviewers: Miriam Cooley, Acadia University; Bill Gadsby, University of Winnipeg; and David Friesen, University of Regina. Thanks as well to our secretaries for preparing the manuscript and knowing when we needed their assistance. Our thanks are extended especially to Bev Tomlinson, Frances McSephney, and Shelley Clark.

We are grateful for the Social Sciences and Humanities Research Council of Canada, whose support of the project *Teaching and Learning: Articulating A Knowledge Base for Teacher Education* provided the stimulus for this book. And last, but certainly not least, we wish to thank our editor, Tammy Scherer, for her insightful comments and pleasant manner during the process of producing this book.

Foreword

One of the enduring challenges in teacher education is to involve cooperating teachers in schools with the teacher education program at the university. The literature describes many attempts to bridge the gap between the more theoretical university program and the more practical school-based activity. One finds examples of field-based programs that "bring" the theory to the school. Conversely, there are examples of school teachers assigned to teacher education programs to bring "the real world of schools" to the more rarefied climate of the university. Since it is inevitable that teacher education programs will include both courses about teaching and education and student teaching experiences in schools, the discussion about the relation of theory and practice in the two venues seems likely to endure. As a consequence, the relation of cooperating teachers to the teacher education program will be problematic.

The issue I posed in the previous paragraph is a real one, but the way I have framed it might well be profoundly misleading. In what I said above, I assumed that theory and practice have physical locations. Theory is what happens in teacher education institutions and practice is what happens in schools. I believe, as well, that this is a common assumption. It lies behind the often-heard statement to student teachers that, "You can forget what you learned at university. The school is the real place for learning how to teach." But theory and practice are constructions of the human mind; they are not the sorts of things that have physical locations. It is more helpful to think of theory and practice as two different but related ways of solving problems. Theoretical thinking arises out of practical issues, and determining practice can be the implementation of theoretical positions. Rather than a dichotomy or an *either/or* between theory and practice, we can see them as two related ways of describing the problems and issues that teachers and educators face. Both help us address the difficulties and challenges we face in education. And, most importantly, they do not become the special properties of different classes of people.

When we think of theory and practice along the lines just described, it becomes immediately apparent that the division of labor in teacher education between universities and schools is not that one has a hold on theory and the other on practice. Instead, we see naturally that both can contribute to theory and practice, and that university professors and cooperating teachers are equal partners in the teacher education enterprise.

There are many challenges to teacher education programs when we conceptualize teacher education as involving university-based and school-based teacher educators as partners. Not the least of these is communication. The university-based personnel are relatively few in numbers and typically work in close proximity to one another. Cooperating teachers are greater in number, physically separated and often isolated, and have much less opportunity for contact with their partners in teacher education. This problem is compounded by the assumption among cooperating teachers that it is the university-based program's responsibility to tell them what to do. This view can be reinforced by the not-uncommon attitude of university faculty expecting cooperating teachers to simply implement the university's model of teacher education without question or discussion.

These comments describe the territory and issues that *Learning-to-Teach* covers. Although the authors do not put their subject matter in quite these terms, their description and elucidation of what they call the context of learning-to-teach clearly implies that the concepts of theory and practice suggest different ways of framing issues in teacher education. As well, to put teacher education into the context of a learning community makes all parties involved equal partners. Faculty members, cooperating teachers and student teachers all contribute to the process of becoming a teacher—of the development from neophyte to fully fledged professional.

This book also addresses one of the great challenges of teacher education, that of helping all the partners to understand their distinctive contributions to teacher education and to appreciate the roles and expertise of each. Through the case studies and exercises provided, cooperating teachers, faculty members and students can develop insight into the complex process of becoming a teacher and into the multifaceted knowledge and skills inherent in this demanding task. To become a teacher is both important and difficult. *Learning-to-Teach* will not make this process any easier, but the understanding of teaching displayed here and the material provided to the reader will make the process more straightforward.

Allen Pearson, Dean
Faculty of Education
The University of Western Ontario

EXPLORING LEARNING-TO-TEACH: CONCEPTS, CASE STUDIES, AND CRITICAL INCIDENTS

Chapter

1

The process of teacher development or *learning-to-teach*, is complex and ongoing. It occurs at different times and in different contexts—preservice education, early career supervision, and collaborative professional inquiry. Student teachers and even experienced teachers are always in the process of *becoming*, of trying to develop an identity as a teacher, and of learning more about teaching and learning. What is frustrating and confusing, especially for novice teachers, is that no one knows how to prepare the best teachers, nor has anyone ever clearly explicated how it really happens that novices learn-to-teach or become teachers.

> Teacher education consists of a loosely coordinated set of experiences designed to establish and maintain a talented teaching force for our nation's elementary and secondary schools. The simplicity of this description belies, however, the complexities and contradictions that beset teacher education as an activity of enormous size and diversity. (Doyle, 1990, p. 3)

Central to our work over the last few years has been a commitment to bring together novice teachers, cooperating teachers, and university faculty to inquire into the complexities of the practicum in teacher preparation. In this book, we have attempted to further this agenda in a manner that recognizes the need to bring together the perspectives of all three members of the *practicum triad* (i.e., student teacher, cooperating teacher, and university advisor) to further the understanding, teaching, and practice of learning-to-teach. An ongoing dilemma in teacher preparation is the separation between professional course work in the university and professional practice in the schools. Bringing these two worlds closer has been the focus of a year-long course we have offered for cooperating teachers for the last eight years. This course has provided a forum where we have shared perspectives, debated issues, and inquired jointly

1

into the perennial problems of preparing novice teachers for the classroom. In fact, this book is one outcome of our collaborative inquiry with cooperating teachers in that course.

In this book we explore the complexity of learning-to-teach within the unstable, indeterminate contexts of teaching. Through this inquiry, we promote the development of a reflective stance in learning-to-teach for all of the participants in the practicum triad, bringing novices and teacher educators together into a community of learners. Through the development of concepts related to teaching and learning and their illustration in case studies, we explore the complexity and the context of the simple and modest phrase, *learning-to-teach*. The purpose of this book, then, is to provide opportunities for members of this community of professional practice to think critically about their roles, practices, and influences in learning-to-teach. This discussion is designed ultimately to provide a venue for considering transformation in teacher education.

We begin this chapter by outlining some of the principles we bring to the discussion of learning-to-teach in the current context of teacher education. In our professional practice, we are committed to the concept of a community of learners and we promote the development of a scholarship of pedagogy that student teachers and teacher educators will find useful. We conclude with an activity that we believe encourages readers to begin to articulate and reflect on their own commitment to a community of professional practice.

LEARNING-TO-TEACH

Learning-to-teach is more than just the recollections, observation, study, or practice of teaching strategies; the process requires a deep understanding of principles of learning and the application of those learning principles through practice, self-evaluation, and personal, professional reflection. After spending more than 15 000 hours observing teaching as pupils in elementary and secondary schooling (Lortie, 1975), novice teachers frequently perceive teaching, and subsequently learning-to-teach, as being not very difficult. However, they need to understand that it is both a complicated and time-consuming venture and an active, conscious, and transformative experience.

> Teaching is a highly complex series of acts. It is not learned easily. Further, it cannot be done by formula or recipe. It is idiosyncratic. At the same time it must fit the learner, the context, and the knowledge or skill being taught. Teaching behaviour can seldom be transferred unchanged from one teacher to another. A technique or approach that works for one teacher may not be effective for another. (Huling-Austin, Odell, Ishler, Kay, & Edelfelt, 1989, p. 1)

A preservice program has two distinct but not always inter-related components. One is a practicum in which student teachers observe and practise aspects of teaching in school classrooms for several weeks. The other comprises a university-based component where they study teaching and the principles of learning in a structured and formal professional-school setting. During their preservice year, student teachers are placed for several weeks in school classrooms with experienced teachers (i.e., cooperating teachers) who assume voluntary responsibility for steering them through the early stages of their teacher development. Student teachers usually value their practicum as the most important component in their teacher preparation program and report that in the practicum they really learn about teaching. First-year teachers tell us over and over again that their cooperating teachers were highly influential in their professional growth, and that their cooperating teachers' strategies made a significant impact on their practice in their new classrooms. It seems that cooperating teachers are most willing to pass on the wisdom of their experience, and new teachers are most anxious to receive and practise it. For decades, writers have advocated support programs for cooperating teachers to ensure that the practicum is an educative site for student teachers and that cooperating teachers understand their role as teacher educators. (See for example, Guyton & McIntyre, 1990; Holmes Group, 1986; Royal Commission on Learning, 1994; Zeichner & Liston, 1987). We trust that this book provides both support and insight for cooperating teachers, as well as student teachers and university-based teacher educators.

While the practicum site has a singularly critical impact on new teachers' practices at the beginning of their teaching careers and may, in fact, inhibit new teachers from experimenting with new forms of practice, the value of their university courses are not nearly so clear to student teachers. We contend that the form and substance of the university-based program would be more helpful if it related more closely to their clinical experiences. At the same time, we must also remember that student teachers come to their preservice teacher education programs with preconceptions and negative expectations.

> I don't know what to expect this year as I begin Teacher's College and it's something that I have been thinking a lot about. So many people have told me over the summer that it's a *make work* year—that you don't do anything really important. . . . The feedback that I'm getting from teachers and friends who have been in various teachers' colleges already for a year has been so negative, except for the student teaching part. Practice teaching is supposed to be the really important part of all this. However, I rarely accept anything that someone says at face value—I need to experience it for myself. . . . And I am so keen to become an excellent teacher that I will make this a good year for me (Carlo, student teacher).

As Carlo notes, student teachers are forewarned by professional colleagues and friends to value their classroom experiences, but to devalue their university courses. This advice adds to the controversies surrounding the value of preservice teacher education programs in that these programs are often seen simply as training programs established to prepare new teachers fully for teaching positions in schools rather than as academically based professional programs for novice teachers. The dichotomy between theory and practice is certainly not a new issue, but neither has it abated in spite of growing awareness and literature on the subject. Novices, in order to be successful *teachers*, ultimately, need to understand how knowledge is acquired and how it is used in society. The volume of research that outlines the history of teacher education, the current, popular beliefs about the weakness of current preservice programs, and the concerns of beginning teachers all require that something be done.

> The esteemed model of the teacher has become that of the technologist, technician, or applied scientist. There is little talk . . . about the need for teachers to make critical and informed judgements with respect to both their own practice and what they consider to be the meaning and purpose of education. What is missing from the . . . discourse is the image of the teacher as a transformative intellectual (Giroux & McLaren, 1987, p. 273).

Teachers new to the profession often find themselves socialized into the status quo of a system struggling to respond to changing situations, yet seemingly powerless to bring any change to current practice (Zeichner & Gore, 1990). Teacher educators (both in the schools and the university) need to understand and explicate their own practices if they are to provide student teachers with a basic understanding of educational practice required for taking an active part in educational reform. The development of a collaborative learning environment that promotes reflection on practice either as novice teachers or teacher educators is required if the educational system is to become a community of professional practice.

THE CONTEXT OF TEACHER EDUCATION

The context and subsequent expectations of preservice teacher education programs are described in a variety of ways, depending upon the person speaking—whether student teacher, struggling novice, experienced teacher, administrator, or university teacher educator. Invariably, descriptions about the process of becoming a teacher are vague, frequently negative, divided around the inevitable discrepancy between theory and practice, and often made by people relatively uninformed about the specifics of teacher preparation. Expectations of preservice programs are equally controversial and varied and, again, vary according to the person speaking. For example, student teachers usually expect to see themselves emerge as competent teachers at the end of program. Cooperating teachers and school administrators expect student teachers to learn the essential skills required to confidently handle a full-time teaching position. University-based teacher educators see student teachers as learners and expect their students to engage in the study of education in order to understand the professional milieu they are entering. Although these images and expectations are not totally dissimilar, neither are they necessarily congruent.

At the same time, there are widespread beliefs that inherent and fundamental weaknesses exist in the educational systems of North America and in the professional education of teachers. A number of studies and reports have called for immediate reform in teacher education (Royal Commission on Learning, 1994; Carnegie Forum, 1986; Holmes Group, 1990), yet there is little indication that much has changed. For example, in the province of Ontario, the provincial *Report of the Royal Commission on Learning* (1994) summarizes the popular sentiment that teacher education programs do not prepare beginning teachers well. The commissioners state:

> Pre-service programs are frequently criticized as being too academic and *theoretical* with little opportunity for student teachers in faculties of education to learn from their own experience (Vol. III, p. 15).

They are perceived to be too brief and too shallow to prepare beginning teachers:

> It seems to us that it is an insult to the job of teachers to believe it [how to teach] can be learned in one academic year at a university faculty of education, with perhaps five months of formal instruction and four months of practice teaching, as is presently the case. What is remarkable about the present system is how many teachers cope so well with such limited preparation (Royal Commission on Learning, 1994, p.17).

What is most worrisome, however, is the lack of critical engagement and reflection resulting from the reports' proposals, and the lack of judicious consideration of the complexity of learning-to-teach. As Fraser (1992) has pointed out, this lack of critical engagement has seriously "impoverished the education debate." While we agree that it is vital to improve teacher education programs, we also know that while it is easy to mandate change, it is almost impossible to ensure that it really happens.

After completing their preservice program, most student teachers believe that their first year of teaching will not be too difficult. They tend to make the transition from student teacher to classroom teacher with unrealistic optimism. In a study of 118 beginning teachers, Weinstein (1988) found that her subjects consistently tended to believe they would experience less difficulty than other first-year teachers and that the work of teaching would be less problematic for them than for their colleagues. Critics contend that new teachers have little practical preparation for their first year of teaching and that no other profession purports to expect its newest members to carry out exactly the same tasks on the first day of the job as colleagues with 20 years of experience. The consequences for first-year teachers and the pupils they teach are significant.

> What a year this is! People told me the first year would be difficult but I am finding it almost impossible. They say they have the same expectations for us as for someone with 20 years of experience but that is not true. I think the load they give a first year [teacher] is much heavier and more complicated than that assigned to—*or chosen by*—experienced teachers. I may have the same number of kids in my classes but I have been assigned more of the students with learning problems and more classes where the pupils are struggling. It seems like the senior teachers have first choice in what subjects they teach and the advanced classes, where the teaching is easier, have all been assigned to them, not to those of us in our first year. And I think we are expected to take on more than our share of extracurricular duties than the experienced teachers do. If something comes along at a staff meeting, everyone looks at us (the new teachers) and wonders if we might be interested. Don't get me wrong; I'm not complaining. I would do anything to have a job and I love the school. But the organization and preparation takes so much time. I don't have a life anymore except as a teacher. I have to assume that this is the unspoken *rite of passage* or initiation for new teachers. If you can survive the first year, you will be a successful teacher . . . something I will have to pass on to the rookies when I am the experienced one here (Tarizia, first year teacher).

Teacher education is complicated by the number of stakeholders involved as well as the variety of informed and uninformed opinions that most members of the public have. Difficulties also arise because teacher education programs are implemented at several levels and by several different groups:

- by the university instructors during design and implementation of university courses,
- by cooperating teachers during field experiences that should, but seldom do, relate to university courses, and
- by school administrators who not only select the experienced teachers who will be the school-based teacher educators, but also hire newly certificated teachers and assign them to difficult positions in their first year of teaching.

Typically, student teachers are seen as having little impact on the educational system. Instead, they are conceptualized as "passive receptacles" of expert knowledge (Blackmore & Kenway, 1995) during their teacher education programs. In this book, however, we regard learning-to-teach as a career-long process that becomes more complex and transformative as one develops professionally. We believe that learning-to-teach is never complete and becomes more and more engaging as one becomes involved and committed to membership in the community of professional practice.

TOWARDS A SCHOLARSHIP OF PEDAGOGY

A significant component of our efforts to create a continuing dialogue among teacher educators in universities and schools, is a concept we call a *scholarship of pedagogy* (Geddis, Lynch, & Speir, 1998). As educators, we are concerned about pedagogy at two levels: the teaching of school subject matter to pupils in schools and the teaching about this teaching to novice teachers in teacher preparation programs—what we are labelling learning-to-teach.

In both cases, we are committed to a serious, detailed and critical study of pedagogy by a community of university-based and school-based teachers. Such study, as Shulman (1999) points out, is legitimately referred to as *scholarship* when: (i) it is conducted in public, (ii) it is subject to the critical review and evaluation of other members of the community of inquiry and (iii) community members begin to use, modify and build upon the products of other community members' scholarship (p. 15). As will become apparent in Chapter 3 and throughout the book, we view professional practice as best guided by both the practical experiential knowledge of practitioners and the formal theoretical knowledge of researchers. Unlike the technical view, which regards teaching as the *application* of formal theoretical knowledge, we see teaching as a far more complex endeavour. It is a process in which practitioners draw on formal theory, practical experience, and their knowledge of learners and learning contexts to design learning activities. Integral to this creative design process is teacher *reflection*—deliberation about means, ends, and the broad consequences of pedagogical interventions for pupils and society.

Much of the practical expertise of teachers in schools and universities is tacit in nature—i.e., most practitioners would be hard pressed to articulate what they know about teaching or how they learned it. Consequently, an essential part of a teacher educator's inquiry is the *surfacing*—i.e., making explicit—of their own tacit understandings so that they can make them available to others. Essential to this process is the acquisition of a language to represent and communicate the complexities of a variety of incidents of teaching practice. As Jackson (1968) noted more than 30 years ago, one of the most notable features of teacher talk is the absence of professional language that adequately captures the complexity of pedagogical practice. We would suggest that little has changed in the intervening years. Therefore, one aim of this book is to develop a shared language adequate to support our notion of a scholarship of pedagogy.

To foster this scholarship of pedagogy, we introduce in each chapter conceptual frameworks that we feel have the potential for illuminating significant issues in teaching and learning-to-teach. It is our intention that readers will explore these concepts in context when they come to the case studies, which follow the conceptual framework in each chapter. Then they can conceptualize problems, design solutions, and deliberate about consequences—intended and unintended.

USING CASE STUDIES

Essential to our inquiry into learning-to-teach is the production of detailed, well contextualized accounts of teaching that can be studied, analysed, and shared with others. The case studies are examples—most of them in the context of learning-to-teach—of the kinds of accounts that have been developed in collaboration with cooperating teachers. From our perspective, such case studies provide essential material, not only for experienced professionals' critical scrutiny of their own and their colleagues' teaching practices, but also for novice teachers' development of their own skills, dispositions, and knowledge required to learn to think and act like a teacher. In general, the case studies set the contexts and frameworks of teaching and learning in vignettes of real practice and they present examples of practice in the messy and complicated world of day-to-day professional work. Educational dilemmas do not happen in neat, tidy boxes, which pertain to specific issues. Rather, teachers often find themselves entwined in a dozen quandaries at the same time. For example, during student teaching sessions, cooperating teachers find themselves involved in typically busy, everyday school affairs, and their work with student teachers can become an unsupported burden on top of their full-time responsibilities. Just trying to sort out the strands of each little difficulty can provide an additional source of frustration. While there are no "right answers" to the problematic situations in the case studies (which you will read about in Chapter 4), some solutions are better than others.

Case studies help novice teachers and teacher educators transform their tacit understanding of learning about teaching into explicit forms of knowledge. In our experience, better practice can develop from a clearer understanding of theory and this process, in turn, provides (through guided discussion) opportunities for theory to grow out of practical dilemmas. We have chosen the case studies specifically because they document practice with student teachers, and because they create opportunities to engage teacher educators and novice teachers in analysing problems. To be effective, this analysis needs to focus both on devising strategies for resolving the problematic situation and on critiquing the utility of a variety of theoretical notions for illuminating teaching and learning-to-teach. Thus, these cases are written to allow cooperating teachers, student teachers, and faculty members to have opportunities to articulate and discuss their beliefs and practices of learning-to-teach in the context of lived experience. They offer opportunities both for learning-to-teach and for understanding and improving the process.

The cases are all based on actual experiences and have been shared with the authors by student teachers, cooperating teachers, and university faculty as describing significant issues which they have faced in field experiences. The cases are not *typical examples* of practice, but rather typical of the types of problems that practicum participants have experienced. Issues of learning and teaching have been intentionally set in the context of real classrooms to capture the emotional involvement of the participants. And, while the cases have been chosen to allow class discussions to focus on a particular aspect of the supervision process, they include other relevant issues, which reflect life in real classrooms. In order to work through the cases, participants will have to deal with primary and secondary issues as they emerge. The cases invite readers

- to engage in discussions of the various problematic situations
- to frame these as particular problems
- to examine alternative solutions to problems
- to critically reflect on their personal practice.

We trust that readers will use the conceptual frameworks provided prior to the case studies as *lenses* through which to view the cases from different perspectives.

By now it should be apparent that we see both the conceptual frameworks and the case studies as essential to our stated purpose of developing a means for reconceptualizing the ways in which teachers learn-to-teach. We expect that by employing the conceptual frameworks in analyzing the case studies our readers will not only find them useful, but also will modify and supplement them to more adequately deal with the situations portrayed. In doing so, they—whether novice teacher or teacher educator—will be engaging in the pedagogical inquiry so central to the practice of thoughtful teachers. We anticipate that this experience will prompt them to join our community of pedagogical inquiry and make their own contributions to the emerging scholarship of pedagogy. Finally, the effective use of these cases requires all participants in the discussions to be open, respectful, encouraging and receptive to other perspectives, while recognizing that teacher-learners are the only ones who have real control over their own professional learning (Harrington, 1991).

Critical Teaching Incidents and Learning-to-Teach

In order to begin the process of, and to promote the kind of, learning-to-teach that we advocate, we are ending this introductory chapter with a personal response activity that we refer to as a Critical Teaching Incident (see Figure 1.1). Learning-to-teach requires deliberation and action that takes the learner beyond factual recall of *prima facie* information or the experience of a situation, and toward the critical articulations that emerge from a scholarship of pedagogy. This activity requires an expressive and secure climate in which novices and teacher educators can further their own learning-to-teach by examining detailed and well-contextualized critical incidents—incidents that provoked wonder, angst or ambivalence for others learning to teach. Requiring participants to explicitly articulate a situation by writing it down to analyse the activity allows for personal and interpersonal discussion and growth. For example, a description may result in discussion participants looking at the incident differently as they attempt to discern what has made the particular situation significant. When articulated in this way, the incident becomes a vignette or miniature case study, which can be shared with other teacher-learners in a search for creative solutions. Through the course of this activity, a community should begin to be developed—a community of professional practice comprised of novice and experienced teachers, a community in which participants will feel free to share personal, professional experiences in a respectful, supportive learning environment.

Various groups will articulate the critical incidents in ways as diverse as the individuals in the community. This complexity is part of the value of the methodology in learning-to-teach that we espouse. Once detailed, the teacher-learner can use this personal case to analyse and reflect on the situation personally or learn through interaction with others analysing their own or others' experiences. In summary, then, the Critical Teaching Incident activity is an exercise, which provides an opportunity for learning teachers (whether student teachers, cooperating teachers or university-based teachers) to engage in articulation and communication as rooted in their personal experiences of learning-to-teach.

The following guidelines may help in completing this exercise.

- Select a teaching incident that was important to you because it either increased your understanding of teaching and learning or invoked questions about the teaching and learning process. It does not matter whether you were the major participant or if you describe an incident that happened to someone else.

- Use the headings on the Critical Teaching Incident (Figure 1.1) as a guide to help you describe what happened. Include as much detail as possible so as to recall as rich a context as possible.

- After completing the Critical Teaching Incident, consider ways of reframing the situation or viewing it from someone else's perspective (e.g., a pupil, another teacher, a parent, and a principal). Did the reframing change how you viewed the situation in any way? If so, describe the changes.

- Describe how you might use this situation to help someone else (e.g., a novice teacher) better understand teaching. What aspects of teaching and learning will the new teacher have to grasp in order to make sense of the incident and to appreciate its significance? How does this situation relate to theory and practice?

For next class

FIGURE 1.1   Critical Teaching Incident

Consider an event related to your own experience in teaching that seems important and describe the incident in as much detail as you can in point form. If you have some second thoughts as you go along, just include them.

The following outline may help you capture the details of the event but use it only as a guide. There is no need to adhere to a category if it is not useful.

a)   Describe the context

b)   What were your intentions?

c)   Who was involved?

d)   What did you do?

e)   What happened as a result?

f)   How did the events make you rethink your views of teaching, learning, pupils, subject matter, etc.?

g)   Further comments (e.g., future expectations, predictions, what you learned . . .)

THE CONTEXT OF LEARNING-TO-TEACH

In a very real and immediate sense, prospective teachers *know* the professional context of teaching. This occurs because teaching, unlike practising medicine, law, or journalism, happens in a context with which we have personal familiarity. Today, with more and more children exposed to some sort of preschool experience, their initial socialization into the norms and practices of the classroom can begin as early as age three. By the time prospective teachers commence their professional preparation, they have spent a major portion of their lives in close proximity to teachers.

When we watch doctors, lawyers, and journalists in television shows or in movies, we vicariously experience the emergency rooms, courtrooms, and newsrooms. Our understanding of classrooms, however, is much more immediate. We smell the chalk dust, feel the anxiety of not knowing the answer, and revel in the satisfaction of solving a difficult problem. This long *apprenticeship of observation* (Lortie, 1975) has profound consequences. In effect, novice teachers have been learning about teaching for a long time, and come to their professional teacher preparation knowing a great deal. Some of their information will be very helpful; some will be incomplete or even erroneous—eventually producing anxiety and even impeding their professional growth. This *problem of familiarity* underlies many of the problems that confront beginning teachers.

THE PROBLEM OF FAMILIARITY

The roots of the problem of familiarity lie in the point of view these very experiences create. Novice teachers' long *apprenticeship of observation* has been from the perspective of *student* and, as we will describe shortly, *generally successful students*. When they move to the other side of the teacher's desk, their perspective is fundamentally altered. As pupils, they simply accepted the cheerful, organized environment of Ms. French's grade 5 class and their own developing sense of competence as *just the way things are*. They didn't notice how she selected particular learning tasks to stretch children already reading well beyond their grade level, and different tasks to challenge but not frustrate children still struggling to decode individual words. They were blissfully unaware of how Ms. French's expertise in selecting instructional tasks was so fundamental to the smooth way in which her classroom ran. Disruptions, to which bored, bright children or frustrated, struggling children sometimes resort, did not occur. All looked so easy, and no doubt, they could see themselves—just like Ms. French—as the centre of a happy, productive learning community. Spectators often unwillingly underestimate the expertise of the players, and Ms. French herself may have contributed to her pupils' devaluing of her accomplishments. Teachers not infrequently deflect comments about their accomplishments with remarks like, "Well you know this year's grade 5s really are exceptional."

One consequence of the problem of *familiarity* for learning-to-teach is that novice teachers typically hold unrealistically optimistic views of how well they will perform in the classroom. Generally, prospective teachers enter their teacher education programs with a high degree of confidence in their ability to teach. As one teacher interviewed by Crow (1987) put it:

> I feel comfortable about being a teacher . . . it's natural. . . . I don't feel that's it is new. I know how classrooms operate and . . . I'm sure I could do a better job, right now as a teacher than most of what I see out there now (cited in Weinstein, 1989, p. 53).

When early practicum experiences disconfirm novice teachers' expectations, they suffer considerable anxiety. Typical responses involve blaming themselves—"I guess I'm not really cut out to be a school teacher"—or blaming the pupils (and the cooperating teacher)—"What makes pupils think that they can behave like this?" From our perspective, a more fruitful approach involves developing an awareness that learning to teach is more complex and demanding than it first appears, and paying explicit attention to the question of what constitutes realistic aspirations at different points in professional development.

A DEVELOPMENTAL PERSPECTIVE ON PROFESSIONAL GROWTH

The process of learning-to-teach can usefully be thought of in terms of three developmental stages. Initially, novices are concerned with "simply coping," then with "looking like teachers," and finally, with fostering their pupils' learning. Our developmental perspective on professional growth (see Figure 2.1) is not meant to imply that there are fixed stages that novices must go through or that expert teachers are consistently functioning at "higher levels" of professional competence. It is meant to be suggestive rather than prescriptive. Teaching is a complex, multifaceted enterprise, and learning-to-teach is, if anything, more complex. The three stages we set out in our developmental perspective are meant to suggest foci of preoccupations, activities, and concerns that characterize qualitatively different kinds of professional practice. While, ultimately and ideally, we aspire to foster student learning, many factors may restrict our practice. In particular, when we—whether novice or expert—move into new teaching contexts—we need to acquire a great amount of contextual knowledge in order to function effectively. For novice teachers this is often accompanied by considerable anxiety about being regarded as less than competent by pupils and their

---

FIGURE 2.1   A Developmental Perspective on Professional Growth

1. **Initial coping**
   - need to learn about pupils, classroom routines, teaching strategies, curriculum, and school culture
   - focus on *getting through the lesson*
   - experience *reality shock*

2. **Taking on the professional role**
   - focus on self and *teaching*
   - concern with external evaluation—"Am I doing it right?"
   - learning to get and hold pupils' attention, lead students through activities, and keep students on task

3. **Fostering pupil learning**
   - focus on pupils and their learning
   - experiment with diverse teaching strategies
   - reflect on consequences of learning for students in the short and long term
   - reflect on consequences of learning for society

---

cooperating teachers. One thing that this developmental perspective can do for novice teachers is to relieve this anxiety.

Initial Coping

Because of their familiarity with the teaching context and their considerable confidence, novice teachers frequently experience some sort of *reality shock* early in their practicum. The anxiety of reality shock can be quite overpowering. In the first few weeks of student teaching, novice teachers typically suffer considerable tension and anxiety. In one study, novices reported "walking around like zombies," "not being able to sleep at nights," "waking up at three in the morning, pacing the floor, reciting lessons for the next day." One student teacher even reported being physically sick every morning for the first two weeks (Calderhead, 1987, p. 271). These novices identified their anxieties as being rooted in three different areas. First was the stress of the classroom situation itself, where they were responsible for maintaining discipline among 30 or more pupils and directing their learning. Second was the stress of continually being "on view" and evaluated. Third, and perhaps most significant, was the shock of discovering that their conceptions of teaching did not match the reality they faced each day.

Novice teachers begin teacher preparation with ideal conceptions or images of the teaching role and of teacher-pupil relationships. Typically, they view the role as that of guide and friend, and the relationship between teacher and pupil as one of warmth, cooperation, and mutual respect. Their idealized view of the teacher role can contrast sharply with what they perceive to be happening in the classroom role of their cooperating teachers. Novices have described their cooperating teachers as "disciplinarians," "unnecessarily strict," and even as "tyrants" and "ogres" (Calderhead, 1987, p. 271). However, as they take on the task of getting and holding the attention of 30 or more pupils, novice teachers typically find themselves adopting more of an authoritarian persona that includes a focus on maintaining order, a distrust of pupils, and a punitive, moralistic approach to pupil control. This gives rise to one of the fundamental challenges of learning to teach—i.e., coming to terms with the complex issues of classroom control while still sustaining an image of teaching that is compassionate, respectful, and committed to the interests of pupils.

Taking on the Professional Role

During student teaching, the overarching concern of novices is demonstrating their competence to assume the role of teacher in their own classroom. Cooperating teachers and novices alike are well aware that Student Teaching Reports play an extremely important, if not pivotal role, in the hiring process. Consequently, there is a (quite legitimate) focus on the novice acquiring those external behaviours that can be viewed as characterising the competent teacher. The danger here is in adopting an excessively *utilitarian perspective on learning-to-teach* that motivates the novice to adopt strategies that "work" with little concern for the broader ethical and political dimensions of teaching. Ironically, it is frequently ethical and political concerns that have provided the impetus for novice teachers to embark on a teaching career in the first place.

Central to *looking like a teacher* are the classroom management tasks of getting and holding student attention, guiding them through learning activities, and keeping them on task. The fundamental challenge during this stage of learning-to-teach is acquiring good management skills while keeping student learning front-and-centre. This is not easy because novice teachers are strongly motivated to "succeed" and to be accepted by professional colleagues, which leads them to imitate the successful strategies employed by successful teachers. While modelling (by cooperating teachers) and imitation (by novice teachers) are central strategies of learning-to-teach in the practicum, two pitfalls are associated with them. First, novice teachers interpret both *success* and the observed teaching in terms of what they (as novices) experience—i.e., through their novice teacher conceptions of teaching, learning, and subject matter, which act as filters through which they see their cooperating teachers' practice. Second, an overemphasis on modelling and imitation can lead to a deadening pattern of uncritical uniformity and the cultural maintenance of teaching practices—practices that may not meet the changing needs of an increasingly diverse population.

Fostering Pupil Learning

Teaching is intractably bound up with the intention to promote pupil learning. All pupils, however, do not learn at the same rate or in the same way; nor do they bring the same experiences to their learning. Fostering pupils' learning in the classroom involves monitoring their responses to a learning activity and then providing prompts, adjusting the activity, or re-teaching prerequisite learnings, etc., in response to individual pupil's difficulties. These types of teacher responses to children's efforts move teaching beyond simply *telling* or *covering the curriculum*. Novice teachers, who themselves have been successful students, do not always find it easy to recognize if or why pupils are having difficulty. Part of what enables experienced teachers to guide pupils in productive directions is their knowledge of those aspects of the subject matter crseating difficulties for pupils, the possible causes of those difficulties, and teaching strategies for potentially overcoming them. This kind of knowledge, involving both pedagogy and subject matter, is called *pedagogical content knowledge* (Shulman, 1987). Pedagogical content knowledge distinguishes the teacher from someone who is simply a subject matter expert. Consequently, acquiring pedagogical content knowledge is a central task in learning-to-teach.

The classroom's inherently complex, indeterminate, and unstable context requires teachers to master a variety of strategies. Russell Ackoff (1979) has referred to similar professional contexts as *messes*—dynamic situations consisting of complex systems of changing problems that continually interact with one another. Consequently, expert teachers do not so much apply a superior technique to a situation, as employ a diverse repertoire of teaching strategies to explore and then respond to the changing learning needs of their diverse pupils. By carefully monitoring how pupils are making sense of and responding to a learning context, expert teachers are able to select teaching moves with the potential to address pupils' learning difficulties. Schön (1983) refers to this monitoring process as *listening to the back-talk* from a situation, i.e., carefully considering the consequences, both intended and unintended, of a teaching move in light of what was intended, and the other teaching moves that could have been made. From this point of view, the teacher can be seen as continually *experimenting*—employing a particular teaching strategy, assessing the consequences, and then continuing, modifying, or replacing the strategy. To carry out this dynamic exploration of pupil learning, the expert teacher relies both on a high level of diagnostic skill and on an extensive repertoire of diverse teaching strategies.

One value of this developmental perspective on professional growth is that it provides a vocabulary for talking about the process of learning-to-teach, or alternatively, acts as a lens through which to view professional development. By suggesting this progression and its three possible stages, we make certain assumptions about the process of learning-to-teach. We also, in a very real sense, make it possible to observe the developmental stages. In some cases, there may well be little evidence of one or more of the three stages suggested. The Initial Coping stage may be severely attenuated because a novice has had experience in a similar context. Not infrequently novice teachers are so caught up in the Taking on the Professional Role stage that they have little opportunity to focus on the learning of their pupils. Our intent is that the conceptual framework will help novices, cooperating teachers, and faculty advisors to observe aspects of learning-to-teach that they might not otherwise have done. At the same time, we hope that it will assist novices and teacher educators in coping with the anxieties and tensions inherent in taking the extended journey of becoming expert teachers.

Conceptual frameworks can be extremely useful in helping us think in more complex and productive ways about teaching and learning to teach. Consequently, before moving on from considering the context of learning-to-teach, we would like to turn our attention to the central concept of the enterprise, *teaching*. Again our intent is suggestive not prescriptive; we hope to provide a description not of *the way to teach*, but rather of *four ways of thinking about teaching*.

FOUR PERSPECTIVES ON TEACHING AND LEARNING

It is difficult, if not impossible, to talk about teaching without talking about learning. Consequently, we will direct our attention to both in spite of the initial confusion this may produce. In addition, while we do not intend to imply that these are the only ways to think

FIGURE 2.2	Four Perspectives on Teaching and Learning[1]		
	Teaching	**Learning**	**Metaphor**
Transmission	telling	remembering	filling up a receptacle
Skill Development	drilling and practising	enhancing performance	athletic training
Natural Development	facilitating growth	growing	gardening: weed, feed, & wait
Constructivist	promoting conceptual change	constructing new knowledge	learning to *see* in new ways

about teaching/learning, we do believe that one or more of these views (see Figure 2.2) underly most discussions of teaching.

Obviously, we are not claiming that any one of these perspectives or theories captures any actual teaching/learning event unequivocally or completely. Classroom teaching is much too indeterminate, complex, and variable. Rather, these four perspectives can help us articulate a range of interpretations that do justice to the ambiguity, complexity, and transient character of the teaching/learning encounter.

Teaching as Transmission of Knowledge

"Teaching as transmission of knowledge" is probably the most widely held view of teaching/learning. It is epitomised by the university lecture with the professor at the lectern, and the students listening intently as they busily take notes. These notes embody the material to be transmitted. Frequently, teachers make notes—either on a blackboard or an overhead transparency—as they lecture. Notes can be seen either as integral to instruction—an aid to students' learning of the subject matter at hand—or as part of a parallel agenda, which focuses on assisting students to become better learners. This parallel agenda might well be used in a Skill Development perspective on teaching/learning; that is, students would be seen as developing the skills needed for producing good notes. The lecture itself, however, can still be seen within an overall Transmission perspective—students needing to develop certain competencies so they can take on the role of learner as prescribed by the Transmission perspective.

The ubiquity of the Transmission perspective can be observed when young children decide to play school. Typically, the child playing the teacher stands in front of her seated pupils while she writes on a blackboard. This view of teaching is so deeply engrained that not following it can be a source of disappointment for some beginning teachers. Student teachers are typically impatient to "take over the class and deliver the lesson." For many, this is what teaching is really about. Monitoring pupils doing seatwork, working with reading groups, or providing individual help with multiplication problems, somehow seems less important to these student teachers. Ironically, these other instructional responsibilities can provide the experience student teachers need to begin to think about teaching/learning in ways other than the transmission of knowledge.

Teaching as Skill Development[2]

Developing a skill usually involves performing a fairly well-defined sequence of activities, a dynamic central in the teaching as skill development perspective. Initially the teacher illustrates the skill—whether it be a tennis serve or solving quadratic equations. Frequently, this includes breaking the skill down into a number of parts, conveying how the parts relate to each other, and describing the expected outcome. Following the teacher presentation, students engage in *guided practice* during which the teacher monitors their performance and gives them feedback intended to remedy their errors and enhance their performance. When students appear to have reached the appropriate level of mastery, they then proceed to *independent practice,* frequently in the guise of *homework*. This independent practice sets the stage for the next day's lesson which often begins with a *review* of the material taught today—frequently facilitated by and combined with the "taking up of homework."

The Skill Development perspective can alert a teacher to students' need to actually engage in an activity if they are to learn to do it. Not only do teachers need to set time aside for practice, but they also need to ensure that pupils are *on-task* and performing the activity correctly. Diagnosing student errors, providing constructive feedback, and developing remedial learning activities are all central components of the coaching role in Skill Development. While the Skill Development perspective can be seen as rooted in the metaphor of the training of athletes, it is much more broadly used. Teachers often base the teaching of mathematics on this perspective, and the classic secondary school mathematics lesson is a good illustration of its use. In elementary schools, teachers use it for a variety of subject matter (e.g., spelling, reading, arithmetic, and music). Its major shortcoming appears to be its inability to articulate more holistic aspects of learning (e.g., developing understanding, and the non-algorithmic design processes involved in composition in the arts, science, and technology).

Teaching as Natural Development

The Natural Development perspective focuses on the children's development as central to any attempt at instruction, stressing that they must be ready for learning. There is little doubt that in a variety of areas, human beings go through developmental processes that involve the unfolding of increased competency. With little direct instruction children learn to grasp objects within their reach, to communicate in their native language, and to walk, run, and climb trees. Certainly the child needs access to models of what it means to speak, walk, and climb for this development to occur—someone to speak to and trees to climb, etc.—and when these models are not present, learning may not occur. However, it appears that the majority of children learn these things with little *explicit teaching*. This view of teaching/learning draws particular attention to the fact that providing instruction before children have developed to a point where they can take advantage of the instruction is probably futile and possibly detrimental. Before children's bone and muscle structures have developed fully, it is impossible to teach them to walk. Attempts to do so could mean running the risk of causing serious damage, physically and emotionally. Research in developmental psychology suggests that as well as developing physically, children also develop cognitively, emotionally, and morally.

Because children progress in stages, teachers work at providing rich learning environments, so when pupils are developmentally ready, the resources they need for learning are available. Educators create cheerful, friendly environments in classrooms with lots of appropriate and appealing books, manipulatives for exploring mathematics concepts, a variety of materials for visual art activities, and perhaps musical instruments or woodworking tools. Most importantly, however, teachers spend considerable time tracking each child's development so that they can provide developmentally appropriate activities for each one. The Natural Development perspective is rooted in a *gardening* metaphor that sees the teacher facilitating the growth of the child much as the gardener cultivating her flowers. The teacher tries to establish an environment that will nurture students' development, weeding out impediments and introducing activities and materials that promote growth. At the same time, the teacher is aware of the need for patience. Just as force-feeding can have detrimental consequences for plant development, too early an introduction to reading, for example, can be detrimental to children's development into adults who can and will read throughout their lives.

Teaching From a Constructivist View

Recently, constructivist perspectives on teaching/learning have gained considerable currency among educational researchers and policy makers. This has been particularly true for those interested in teaching abstract subject matter, especially subjects somewhat removed from the common sense conceptions of everyday life. A considerable body of research has demonstrated that even university graduates retain common sense conceptions of phenomena, which are seriously at odds with the views of scholars in the disciplines they have studied (see e.g., Gardner, 1991). Scientific views of concepts like *animal, fruit, force*, and *work*, differ significantly from their everyday counterparts. More importantly, scientific, mathematical, anthropological, historical, and legal ways of thinking are often fundamentally at odds with the ways of thinking we commonly use every day. The constructivist perspective on learning focuses on the fact that students use the common sense constructs and ways of thinking they bring to the classroom to perceive of and reflect on what they are learning. Pupils are not going to give up these ways of thinking easily; they have developed them over long periods and found them very effective in making sense of their worlds. Teaching intent on helping students to perceive the world in another way needs to pay particular attention to the learners' *preconceptions*—the ideas about subject matter they bring to instruction—and to the way in which these preconceptions act as filters to structure how learners perceive learning activities. Because of the deeply rooted nature of such preconceptions, it is necessary not only to help students become aware of them and how they differ from the conceptual apparatus of the course material, but also to help them see the inadequacies of their current conceptual constructs and the usefulness of adopting new ones. In Piagetian terms, constructivist teaching is teaching aimed not at assimilating new knowledge into learners' present conceptual structures, but at accommodating learners' conceptual structures so they can more adequately deal with novel aspects of the world. Teachers can encourage the dissatisfaction with existing ideas that motivates learners to take on the task of accommodation by using learning activities designed to produce *cognitive dissonance*. Such activities are meant to leave the learner with contradictions that can only be resolved by modifying their existing ideas. While constructivist views of teaching have been widely adopted by teachers of esoteric, abstract subject matter in science and mathematics, they can also bring a fresh perspective to teaching the dispositions and skills essential for democratic group participation (e.g., learning to share, cooperate, and accept difference).

Again, it is important to keep in mind that working from any one of these perspectives can produce learning. Our point is not that any one of these is necessarily better than the others, but rather that teachers need to use a variety of approaches in thinking about what they are doing in the classroom. Their value is that they provide four different ways of thinking about and talking about our instruction in light of the short- and long-term expectations that we have for our pupils' and student teachers' learning.

The case study that follows presents some views of a novice teacher, Kevin, who is in a one-year preparation program, on teaching, students, and subject matter. It has been constructed from data collected during a research study into how novices learn to teach (see Geddis & Roberts, 1998). As you read the study, think about how Kevin's expectations and student teaching experiences relate to your own. Using the two conceptual frameworks presented in this chapter will be helpful.

Kevin's Return to the World of High School

Kevin had been an active high school student with a keen interest in science and mathematics. In university he had initially studied physics and then completed his master's degree in astronomy. While doing graduate work, he worked at the small observatory on campus. He particularly enjoyed the *Saturday Night at the Observatory Program* when the observatory was open to the public. He often gave the short talk that began the program and afterwards, with another graduate student, guided tour groups, demonstrating the equipment and answering questions. Kevin was knowledgeable, articulate, and enthusiastic. During his two years with the program, he gained considerable pleasure from his increasing ability to explain complex scientific topics. By the end of the second year he ran the program on his own.

The September after defending his thesis, Kevin entered the one-year teacher preparation program at the Faculty of Education on the other side of campus. The first few weeks did not really differ much from his previous university experience. He attended large lectures in educational psychology, philosophy, and school and society. He spent about half his class time in methods courses on his two teaching subjects, mathematics and physics. These latter two courses he found more interesting, however, he really wanted to get out into a school and teach. His initial student teaching assignment was a six-week placement at Westwood Secondary School in early October. Westwood, a multi-ethnic school, provided a broad range of programs. Located in the south end of the city, Westwood wasn't quite an inner-city school, but neither was it a suburban school. It did, however, have students with a wide range of needs along with some of the specialized resources necessary to meet those needs. While some students went on to university, the majority went directly to work, or into post-secondary job training at the local community college.

Near the end of the second week of his placement, Kevin's university supervisor Art Johnson arrived at the school to find Kevin and two other student teachers, Maureen and Jin Woo, in the science office discussing classroom management. Art's notes, which follow, provide a flavour of the tensions and anxieties the three were facing.

Kevin was responding to Maureen's point that she was "having troubles" [with discipline], especially with the "bright ones." Kevin allowed that his trouble wasn't with the bright ones but with the others in the class. The trouble, I take it, is the tendency of kids to chat with one another while [the preservice teachers] are trying to teach. Kevin told of telling his group, "I really would like it if you would pay attention, since this is really important material," or words to that effect. He expressed some consternation that this admonition was not very effective. Students were allowed to sit wherever they pleased, but Kevin didn't seem to connect this fact with the chatting and giggling.

What was foremost on [Kevin's] mind, though, was that the students in his class would not treat position as a vector. [A vector is a quantity that has direction as well as magnitude (e.g., 2 kilometres north).] "They don't put on units; they don't use a vector sign." And he has told them "over and over. . . ."

In an effort to suggest a reason for this thick-headedness on the part of his students, I asked Kevin if he recalled Gordon's [his physics methods instructor] discussion to the effect that a lot of physics is counter-intuitive. He recalled that, but disagreed. I indicated that the students had no reason in their everyday world, or everyday language, to think of position as a vector (I gather they do okay with distance), and that it is only in the specialized realm of physics that such an idea is necessary. Kevin didn't respond one way or the other. If this constituted for him a reason for the behaviour of the students, he did not give me any indication.

I asked how his students compared to Arnold's. [Arnold Kent was Kevin's cooperating teacher who taught a parallel physics class.] Kevin indicated that, "[Arnold] allows more chatter than I do." Also, Kevin noted that Arnold didn't "jump in" to correct students as quickly. He also said . . . that Arnold's group is having trouble with position as a vector as well. (Frankly, I found myself wondering why that is such a big deal!)

At that point, I suggested that we should wind up [our interview] to give him time to plan [for his next class]. Kevin's response was that "mechanics is etched into me, so that it isn't a big deal to plan for this afternoon's class." I asked if the textbook treatment was pretty much like he remembers mechanics. He said that he is more comfortable with a more advanced mathematical treatment—the calculus treatment. I then returned to [my earlier] point about this stuff being counter-intuitive, pressing the idea that there needs to be a reason to shift into the physics framework from the ordinary language one. I asked him if all of his students would be taking the senior physics course, and he estimated about 12 or 13 out of 22 based on this year's enrolments of about 40 in this introductory course. [There are two sequential physics courses in the provincial program. The senior course is intended for students who will be going on to university. Kevin is predicting that about half of his course will take the senior physics course.] I then asked why those not going on should bother to learn the stuff. He replied that it was a required course for graduation. (I'm at a bit of a loss on this. I may be a little out of touch with the most recent graduation requirements, but I can't imagine that the senior course in physics would be required for graduation. Kevin wasn't snarky or anything, just matter-of-fact. That's Kevin.)

Finally, I asked Kevin what he had found the most and least useful/interesting/relevant from the in-faculty course work that had proceeded the practicum. He responded (thoughtfully) that the systematic work on lesson planning was very helpful. On the other hand, some of Gordon's "philosophical stuff" was "not very practical."

During a wide-ranging interview after returning to the Faculty, Kevin articulated how he had come to think about the students he had encountered during his student teaching assignment.

Kevin: I had two different classes . . . I taught the one class for about two weeks, switched into the other one for two weeks, and then went back for a couple more weeks to the first class. The first one was a really good class . . . more bright people, outgoing people . . . a relatively polite class . . . and they were more willing to listen. They were willing to give responses and to talk to you

about physics . . . they actually thought about physics! The third period class was dead in comparison. There were a couple of really bright people but they weren't really willing to interact in the classroom . . . and the rest, just didn't want to think during class. They just went there, took their notes . . . and sometimes studied at home . . . sometimes didn't. It was a completely different situation. It was a little bit disappointing. I figure that if you're taking 12A Physics [a university preparation course], you're not just taking it for the credit. You are taking it for a reason . . . at least a little bit of interest. But it seemed like a lot of them were just doing it to get their diploma.

Art: And that is really funny because in the overall scheme of things these kids are really self-selected . . . I mean, they don't need that credit to graduate. . . . It is totally optional for them.[3]

Kevin: I'm not sure why a lot of them took it. . . . A lot of them were . . . deficient in mathematics. It was frightening. . . . Rearranging an equation with four or five terms in it was just impossible for some of them. Rearranging $v = d/t$ was even hard for a couple.

QUESTIONS

Framing Problems and Exploring Solutions

1. In many ways, Kevin seems surprised with the students he has encountered. Why might this be? How do students differ from when you were a student? Explore how Kevin's perception might be affected by how he has changed? His selective memory? The new role that he has taken on?

2. How does Kevin see teaching/learning? What evidence do you have for your view? Compare the views of teaching/learning that Kevin holds for his students learning physics, with the views that he holds for his own learning of learning-to-teach physics.

3. Does the Developmental Perspective on Professional Growth help you in making sense of Kevin's views? Does he seem to be wrestling with specific problems characteristic of one or more of the stages?

4. What interventions might you consider to deal with some of the problems that you see Kevin facing?

Personal Reflections and Connections

1. How do Kevin's experiences reflect your own—either as a student teacher or as a co-operating teacher? How did you deal with them?

2. Use the four perspectives on teaching/learning to explore your own views of teaching/learning. What differences are there between your ideal view and what you are able to accomplish on a day-to-day basis? How does the situation make a difference, i.e., what is to be learned, the context, the student, the teacher?

3. Did the problem of *familiarity* play a role in your own learning-to-teach? How?

Reflections on Learning-to-Teach

1. What is your conception of how people learn-to-teach? What is your rationale for this view? Employ the four perspectives on teaching/learning to articulate your views in greater detail.

2. Reflect on your own teacher preparation program. From the characteristics and structure of that program, which conception of *learning-to-teach* is that program based on?

3. What do you see as the central problems of learning-to-teach? Consider how we might go about beginning to address these problems?

ENDNOTES

1. While there have been a variety of attempts to set out different perspectives on teaching and learning, the reader will find our framework most similar to that of Scardamalia and Bereiter (1989).

2. A great deal of research literature is rooted in this perspective on teaching, much of it under the overall catchphrase "effective teaching." A concise but illuminating account of its main characteristics can be found in Berliner (1988).

3. This is an important point because of Kevin's apparent misunderstanding in the very first interview about the compulsory nature of physics as a subject. Now that he realizes that physics is optional, he appears even more at a loss to explain why some students are taking it.

REFLECTION: CONNECTING THINKING AND ACTING IN PROFESSIONAL PRACTICE

In this book, we advocate a view of professional practice guided by personal experience as well as formal knowledge. Central to the effective use of experience and knowledge is using the process of reflection articulated in this chapter. Some practitioners take a purely technical view of professional practice, seeing teaching exclusively as the *application* of the formal knowledge produced by researchers. We, however, see teaching as a much more complex endeavour that draws on explicit research and experiential knowledge while simultaneously being influenced by varied forms of tacit, intuitive knowledge. In addition, we are committed to the view that professional practice can be improved by *reflection*—a process of deliberating about means, ends, and the broad consequences of our actions for both students and society. In all its forms, we believe learning-to-teach involves skilful action and thoughtful reflection clearly contextualized in real instructional contexts. In these clinical settings, teaching and learning occur on two levels—the classroom level of pupil learning, and the professional level of teacher learning. Reflection is essential at both of these levels. Teacher educators are teaching about the role of reflection in teaching children while simultaneously employing reflection in their own practice. (In Chapter 6, we will further explore how reflection at these two levels can be used to enhance novice teachers' access to their pupils' learning experiences.) Because of the centrality of reflection to teacher development, we will, in this chapter, first articulate our conception of reflection, and then employ a case study to engage readers in reflecting on issues of classroom management, which concern novice teachers. We do not, however, regard reflection as essentially, or even primarily, an instrumental matter concerned only with the means of instruction. Later chapters will illustrate the way in which reflection can bring critical perspectives to bear on classroom practice and the broader societal context in which it is embedded.

ARTICULATING THE COMPLEXITIES OF PROFESSIONAL PRACTICE

We first look at the context of classroom teaching to point out the inadequacy of an "applied science" (technical) view of how formal knowledge influences teaching practice. We then articulate our view of reflection derived from the ideas of Schön (1983, 1987), Schwab (1970), and Dewey (1933), and illustrate this view in an analysis of a case study constructed from a teacher's journal. After that, readers are invited to explore substantive issues in the case and our analysis, and then our articulation of reflection and their own processes of reflective inquiry.

CLASSROOM CONTEXTS: COMPLEX, UNCERTAIN, UNSTABLE, AND UNIQUE

Reflection enables teachers to develop strategies appropriate for the complex and confusing environments in our classrooms. Russell Ackoff (1979) has aptly referred to such professional contexts as *messes*—dynamic situations consisting of complex systems of changing problems that continually interact with each other. A room of 30 (or more) unique learners, all with their own agendas, anxieties, and competencies is hardly the environment in which prescriptions derived from theory, as advocated by the technical approach, are very effective.

While the separation of knowledge from experience in fields such as engineering and clinical medicine have brought major changes to our modern world, such an approach has proved to be less than efficacious in teaching. Engineers go to school to learn the theory about strength of materials, distribution of loads in different kinds of structures, etc. that they can apply relatively unproblematically to build a bridge. They are able to do so, however, because they use relatively homogeneous materials and because they need not worry about girders having different agendas. Yet, even the bridge-building engineer, if she enlarges the context of her problem, may find that there are limitations in a simple applied approach for some issues. What about the utility of the bridge? The town in which a bridge is being built may, for example, suffer from a drastic reduction in population if a nearby auto plant is closed. This would leave the few remaining citizens with an expensive tax burden. Or perhaps the large central towers that support the central span will impede the path of spawning salmon, essentially decimating the highly profitable fishing industry in which a large portion of the bridge users are employed. Thus, even for a bridge builder, the particulars of context can demand more than simple "application of theory."

In classrooms where "materials" are highly heterogeneous and possess wills of their own, we can hardly expect that theory will yield simple workable prescriptions. When we employ knowledge—both formal and experiential—in teaching, we do best to use it to *frame* situations so as to identify certain possibilities for action. We can then consider these possibilities in terms of the possible outcomes—positive and negative—or act on them immediately to see if they can yield an acceptable solution. It is not so much that experienced teachers know *what to do* in advance, but rather that they are keenly tuned to the consequences of what they do do. Schön refers to this process of paying attention to the consequences of classroom action as *listening to the backtalk*. Of course knowing what to do to ameliorate negative consequences, or take advantage of positive consequences, is also a central component of teacher expertise. Novice teachers, however, often have serious difficulty in reorienting their thinking from a search for *the generic best way to teach a topic* in which individual students, the classroom, or the community are lost to view, to a reflective, iterative approach tuned to the *backtalk* from the unique particulars of context. Without such a reflective orientation, novice teachers (and other educational practitioners) too often flee from the field of practice in search of some new *high-tech* solution that will provide a *one-size-fits-all strategy* which will spare them the continuing work of learning the particulars of individual students, schools, and communities. All too often, such searches lead, not to the Holy Grail of the *perfect teaching strategy*, but to the rejection of "imperfect" students as illustrated by Kevin in the case study of the previous chapter.

REFLECTION-IN-ACTION: DEALING WITH MESSES

Although teachers cannot unthinkingly rely on the straightforward use of theory as implied by the *applied science* view of practice, competent professionals still exhibit high degrees of expertise in complex environments. Central to an explanation of these spontaneous intuitive performances of competent professionals is what Schön calls *reflection-in-action*. Out of necessity, much of what experienced classroom teachers do involves tacit procedures that effectively manage the flow of ordinary classroom events. What distinguishes reflective practitioners is their ability to respond to events that stand out from this normal flow. Prompted by a problematic event, the reflective teacher is able to surface and assess the insights they have developed because of repeated experiences of practice. Then, by a process of *reframing* they make new sense of the problematic situation and respond in a different way.

Reflection-in-action deals with the unique events of practice by means of *frame experiments*. These involve the use of what Schön has called an *exemplar,* or Barnes (1992), a *frame*. Reflective teachers possess extensive repertoires of exemplars, which they use to frame new situations. Confronted with a novel situation, they focus on an aspect it shares with an exemplar they have dealt with successfully in the past. They then frame the new situation in terms of this exemplar. As well they note similarities and differences and consider the possible courses of action, which the similarities suggested in light of the differences. These *thought experiments* provide reflective teachers with a considered basis for the preliminary actions that follow. The actions in turn function both as *probes* for exploring the new situation and as *moves* for shaping it. Reflective practitioners both think about and act on novel situations. More importantly, however, they "listen to the backtalk," i.e., they consider carefully the consequences, both intended and unintended, of their framing of the situation, and then reframe the situation in terms of other exemplars that may yield more appropriate consequences. This process of framing and reframing yields a variety of possible strategies from which to choose and a reserve of alternative strategies on which to draw. (Sometimes situations are framed, not as problems that can be solved, but as dilemmas that must be managed. We will discuss these ambivalent situations in more detail in Chapter 4.) We see the development of different ways of framing classroom situations to be a central focus for any effort to improve classroom instruction.

CLASSROOM FRAMES

A frame or exemplar consists of two interacting components. One is a *descriptive conceptual scheme* that enables teachers to see classroom events in a particular way; the other is a *script*, which provides organized patterns of action arising from that way of seeing. In a very real sense frames consist of the "default settings" we use to organize both our knowledge of the world and our behaviour in it. The frames we bring to a context enable us to categorize and interpret what we perceive, while simultaneously providing us with congruent ways of acting. Frames fill in situations with aspects of their contexts that the individual has not consciously perceived (Barnes, 1992, p. 16). Frames delineate the features of a situation to be attended to, and consequently the direction of any attempt to change it. In framing a situation in a particular way, we delineate what is to be taken as the problem in the situation and consequently the range of solutions that will be considered (Schön 1983, p. 165). Reframing a situation in an other way delineates different problems and different potential solutions. As a result, it expands the possible actions available to the practitioner struggling to act responsively and responsibly.

Schön's reflection-in-action provides a compelling conceptualization of the spontaneous intuitive performance of the skilled practitioner; it does not, however, clearly articulate how that performance might be modified to deal with new concerns and expectations. Most attempts to assist teachers to modify existing practice involve a more leisurely after-the-fact reflection referred to as *reflection-on-action*. Teachers thinking about today's class, or workshop participants intent on modifying instructional programs, typically engage in reflection-on-action not reflection-in-action. While reflection-in-action and reflection-on-action are similar in form—both involve framing and reframing—they occur over very different time frames. Reflection-in-action occurs in "real time." Teacher responses need to be virtually instantaneous. Reflection-on-action is not subject to such a temporal imperative. Reflection-in-action relies on classroom frames becoming such an integral part of a teacher's performance that the person has little awareness of either the frames or the process, i.e., both the frames and the process are *tacit*. In contrast, reflection-on-action involves a deliberate choice and use of a variety of frames. Both frames and process are *explicit*. The difference is like the contrast between a professional tennis player's backhand return of her opponent's shot, and the studied efforts of a novice to execute the same shot. The professional focuses on winning the point; the novice focuses on executing the backhand.

In order to develop a truly functional frame it is necessary to see events in a particular way and also to act in a manner congruent with that view. If either component is missing, the result is a flawed performance displaying either discontinuity between professed aims and practice (inappropriate action component), or application of routines with inadequate attention to the back talk (limited conceptual component). In reality, the conceptual and action components are complexly interconnected. For analytical purposes, however, separation of the two provides a useful perspective on the potential of reflection-on-action for changing practice. Reflection-on-action has considerable potential to help us shape the conceptual component of our frames; it lets us explore how they bring into focus different facets of classroom experience. Reflection-on-action, however, does not engage us in actually reshaping or replacing our classroom scripts. Consequently, we should expect even after considerable reflection-on-action, to experience difficulties acting in ways congruent with our revised intentions.

Readers should keep in mind the limitations of reflection-on-action in using this book. Due to the limitations of the format, we will be engaging you primarily in reflection-on-action. The task of developing classroom scripts, congruent with the conceptual perspectives the book should help you develop, is essentially your own.

USING CASE STUDIES: AN ILLUSTRATION OF FRAMING AND REFRAMING

When problematic situations emerge from the normal flow of classroom events, they frequently indicate a need to seek information. New information acts as a catalyst that can enable the teacher to reframe the situation in ways that reveal new possibilities for action. The following case study uses a number of entries from Rabea's teaching journal; they illustrate her continued search for both new information and new ways of framing a problematic situation.

Dealing With Bernie

Rabea had taught in the Lancaster District School Board since she left the Faculty of Education eight years ago. In September, she transferred from her previous school in the relatively affluent north end of the city to Jones Avenue in the south. Jones Avenue is an older school in a predominantly working-class neighbourhood. While the school population had been primarily white Anglo-Saxon, there has been a recent influx of new Canadians from Southeast Asia and the Caribbean. For the last three years Rabea had enjoyed having student teachers from the Faculty of Education, so she eagerly agreed when asked to do so again. However, the first few weeks at Jones have been trying, and she has been reconsidering the wisdom of taking on student teachers with this particular grade 3 class.

Rabea's journal

4:00 p.m., Tuesday, September 12

Bernie certainly was a handful today. He seemed even worse than usual. Neither Rebecca nor Lina could get any work done because of his disruptive behaviour. As the day went on, the two girls seemed to be getting more and more frustrated with him. I seemed to be reprimanding him every time I turned around. And

keeping him in to clean out the hamster cage turned out to be more punishment for me than for him. Perhaps I need to put him at a table by himself. At least that way, Rebecca and Lina will get their work done. Certainly, I have to do something. Things cannot go on like this. Tomorrow I need to keep an eye on him to see if I can find out what is going on.

Noon, Wednesday, September 13

Bernie was upset when he arrived this morning. He was 15 minutes late, and couldn't settle down. I was very annoyed—everything had been going so well before he arrived. It seems to me that this has occurred before when he has been late. Perhaps making such a big deal about it wasn't the best strategy. It certainly didn't seem to help him settle down. In fact, he appeared to take a certain satisfaction in the disruption. It is almost as if his behaviour is worse on the days that he is late.

4:00 p.m., Wednesday, September 13

The more that I think about it, the more I am convinced that there is a connection between Bernie's disruptive behaviour during the day and his arriving late . . . Perhaps something is happening at home. On the other hand, I do seem to rise to the bait. I really did overreact this morning to the way he strolled in—as if we were all supposed to pay attention because *he* had arrived. The rest of the class just ate it up. I need to try something different tomorrow. Perhaps he just needs to know that we accept him.

Noon, Friday, September 15

Well Bernie was late again today. However, my brief talk with him seemed to make a difference to his behaviour during the rest of the day. I didn't realize that his mother was in the hospital, so that he has to more-or-less get himself off to school in the morning. It must be difficult for a ten-year-old to deal with the anxiety of a parent's serious illness.

An Analysis

From the entries in Rabea's journal it is apparent that between Tuesday and Friday Rabea had changed the way in which she *framed* Bernie's persistent tardiness. On Tuesday she focused on Bernie's grand entry and its disruptive effect. She saw his repeated transgressions of classroom norms and the detrimental effect that they had on other students' opportunities to learn. Taking seriously her responsibility to provide an orderly learning environment for all students, she saw the need for Bernie to learn that he could not continue this sort of disruptive behaviour. Requiring Bernie to clean out the hamster cage had seemed like a good way to help him learn that he could not behave irresponsibly without suffering some sort of consequence. However, it had little effect other than to make him more resentful. Bernie showed little understanding that his behaviour had unfairly disturbed

other students. She considered isolating Bernie at a desk by himself. While this strategy might appear to have much to recommend it in terms of classroom operation, it would do little to help Bernie learn how to interact appropriately. Isolation might seem like an improvement over cleaning out the hamster cage; however, it would appear to emerge from the same—or at least similar—way of *framing* rooted in the teacher's responsibility for maintaining order.

Rabea's decision to observe more closely the context in which Bernie acts out, led to a fundamental *reframing* of the situation. Her attention to the *back-talk*—Bernie's lack of contrition and continued disruption—led first to an effort to gather more information about the context of Bernie's disruptive behaviour and eventually to a dramatic *reframing* of its significance. Noticing that Bernie's disruptive behaviour appeared to occur on days when he was late for class, and that he "seemed to take a certain satisfaction" from being reprimanded, Rabea decided not to play the tough cop role. Consequently, when Bernie was late on Friday, she took him aside and talked with him. After learning of his mother's illness, Rabea helped Bernie move into a group investigating aircraft in preparation for the next week's unit on transportation. She knew he was interested in aircraft and would have a lot to contribute. A short while later, she was pleased to see Bernie deeply engaged in constructing a poster illustrating the relative sizes of different passenger aircraft.

Thinking About Our Analysis

We have presented Rabea's experience with Bernie as an example of *framing and reframing*—a central component of *reflection-in-action*—showing how teachers develop their own practical theory about what they do. Both beginning and experienced professionals affirm the importance of *learning by experience*, and so it seems particularly important to have a way of talking about how it occurs. Without this, it would be all too easy to fall back on a naive sink or swim view of learning-to-teach.

Rabea's experience with Bernie could also have been presented—and usually is—from an *applied science* perspective on practice. This technical point of view might frame Rabea's situation in terms of broad generalizations about classroom management and control (e.g., "Don't embarrass a student in front of her/his peers," or "Employ consequences that arise naturally from the misdeed.") Given such principles, which might even be substantiated by formal research, Rabea could be trained to more effectively reprimand deviant students. Such a perspective is cognizant with a focus on *effective teaching strategies* for improving classroom practice. Important as developing expertise in effectively reprimanding students might be, we think that such a focus by itself obscures the central core of *professional practice*. Even if Rabea became the district expert in *classroom management*, she would not necessarily be a competent professional. In fact, her expertise in classroom management would undoubtedly predispose her to see disruptive classroom events as issues of management and control—a case of the fallacy, "I have a hammer, and therefore the whole world must consist of nails." What is more central is Rabea's ability to make judgements about how best to act in a given instructional context and to re-evaluate them. We think Schön's view of reflective practice succeeds in helping us start to think about how we engage in this process by *framing* and *reframing* the specific instructional contexts. From such a perspective, the core of increased professional competence is the development of an extensive and diverse repertoire of exemplars that can be used to *frame* and *reframe* the complex, uncertain, unstable, and unique instructional contexts that teachers find themselves in every day. At the same time, we are not implying that developing expertise in areas such as *effective classroom management*, or *cooperative learning* are not important. However, the complex nature of teaching puts the ability to become an expert in all relevant areas beyond the capability of any human being. What is important, is understanding the utility of framing an instructional context in diverse ways and learning the skills to put them into practice.

QUESTIONS

Framing, Reframing, and Exploring Solutions

1. How else might this problematic situation with Bernie be framed? Consider the possibility that the root of the problem lies in Bernie lacking socialization skills, or having a learning disability or a physical disability, or being provoked by one of the other children.

2. For each of the ways you frame the situation consider: (i) what is then seen to be the *problem*; (ii) what actions you could take to test the plausibility of this framing, and (iii) a number of possible solutions to the *problem* along with their feasibility and unintended effects.

Personal Reflections and Connections

1. Recall any personal experiences in which a teacher treated you in a way that was at odds with how you saw the situation. Consider why the teacher might have framed the situation in the way in which she/he did? Why did you frame it differently? What actions (if any) might you have taken to try and resolve the differences in your framing of the situation? What actions might the teacher have taken? (Was the teacher even aware of the disparity in your perceptions?)

2. Try to recall an occasion when you fundamentally changed your view of a situation in which you were involved (in or out of school). Why might you have initially framed the situation differently? What motivated your reframing? Faced with a similar situation in the future, how might you actively search for alternative framings of the situation?

Reflections on Learning-to-Teach

1. Some aspects of learning-to-teach involve learning to apply theory or general principles. Should initial teacher preparation limit itself to this sort of training? Why or why not?

2. Consider the role of the teacher in educational systems driven by an applied science view. Within such a system, can we consider teachers to be professionals? Why or why not?

3. What are the professional consequences for teachers who adopt the reflection-in-action view of professional expertise presented in this chapter?

I Want to Understand It Now! Coping With Pupil Frustration

Fatima was bright, enthusiastic, and energetic. She had always enjoyed school so her parents and friends had not been surprised when she had decided to become a teacher. An excellent student, she had little difficulty in maintaining a straight "A" average throughout her undergraduate degree in psychology. The course work in the first three months of her teacher preparation program had been interesting but not overly demanding, and her first placement in a primary classroom in an inner city school had gone smoothly. She was, however, quite pleased to be placed at Fairview Public School for her second placement. Fairview was located in a relatively affluent suburb. Students came from a variety of ethnic backgrounds, but by far, the majority came from professional families, much like her own. She was looking forward to a very successful practicum.

What follows is Fatima's account of an experience that really made her think about the complexity of teaching and what was involved in becoming a competent professional. It was one of those "Critical Teaching Incidents" that her faculty advisor had talked about. (She had even used his handout to try and capture as accurately as possible what had happened.)

The Context

It was my second day of student teaching at Fairview School. This was going to be a particularly rewarding experience for me because my cooperating teacher, Brenda Proser, and her class were part of an alternative program called PPAL (Parents Participating in Active Learning Program). This program was committed both to active learning on the part of children and to extensive parental involvement in that learning. It made use of individual programming, child-initiated learning, activity centres, and extensive enrichment for all pupils. The class was a four-five-six split grade. Typically, the multiage learning groups into which Ms. Proser organized the children contained pupils from all three grades. One or two parents were in the classroom virtually all the time, and on field trips as many as ten parents could be helping.

On the first day, Brenda assigned me the Enrichment Math Group for the duration of my six-week placement. I was pleased and quite excited at the prospect of having my own group for

the whole practicum. The Enrichment Group consisted of seven pupils, two fourth graders, three fifth graders, and two sixth graders. All were very talented math students, and, as Brenda pointedly told me, did not like to be taught mathematics. They preferred to figure out problems on their own or in small work groups. In spite of differing ages and math backgrounds, they all worked on the same problems.

When math time came, the class split into their respective groups. Hélène, the other student teacher, took a group of grade fours; Brenda took a group of grade fives and sixes; and I took the Enrichment Group. While the other two groups remained at their desks doing seat work, the enrichment pupils worked at a round table in the back corner of the room so they could discuss problems and exchange ideas about solving them.

The Incident

The enrichment pupils quickly joined me at the corner table. Obviously, they were keen to get to work. I handed out the sheet of problems I had prepared on perimeter and area. While some of the questions were quite advanced (e.g., determining the greatest possible area that a given length of fencing could enclose), they could work them out by trial and error and, in the process, get lots of practice on multiplication. I began by cautioning them to read each problem very carefully before attempting to solve it. Quickly and quietly, they got down to work. Everyone seemed to be moving through the problems with ease. There were a few clarification questions, but generally everyone appeared to be having little difficulty.

Then I noticed Susy chewing on the end of her pencil with a very troubled look on her face. She motioned me over to her side of the table. She had become completely stuck on the second problem. I carefully read over the problem with her, asking her to elaborate on how she understood the various bits of information. I then asked her to articulate what the problem was asking her to find. With a little coaching, she came up with a relatively clear problem statement, but then she was stuck. "I have no idea what to do now," she complained. I tried to lead her in the right direction using the hints that had worked with the rest of the group. However, it didn't seem to help. I was peripherally aware that most of the other children had completed the first five problems and were moving on to the final three that I had labelled "advanced." Susy was obviously becoming more and more agitated. I could see the tears welling up in her eyes as she repeated *for the nth time*, "But how am I supposed to know what to do?" Finally after another quite fruitless attempt to take her back through the information given and the question asked, I suggested that she might be better to skip this problem and come back to it later. Wiping the tears from her eyes, she wailed, "But I want to understand it *now!*"

QUESTIONS

Framing, Reframing, and Exploring Solutions

1. Fatima's advice to leave problem 2 and go on to the other problems would appear to be rooted in the view that Susy's agitated state was making it difficult for her to use what she did know to solve the problem. What information would appear to support Fatima's decision to frame Susy's difficulties as affective in nature? What other strategies might emerge from this framing?

2. How else might Susy's difficulties be framed? Might there be particular understandings or skills that she lacked? How might Fatima explore the potential of framing Susy's difficulties as cognitively based? What might she do, if this seemed worth pursuing?

3. How do you think Fatima viewed her teaching role in working with the Enrichment Group? What evidence do you have for your inferences? Might any of the four perspectives on teaching and learning introduced in Chapter 2 assist you in framing Susy's difficulties? Explore any that look promising. What possible strategies do they suggest for Fatima?

4. If students are to work in groups productively, it is important that they be positively interdependent, i.e., they need to work together in ways that promote the learning of all of the group members. Is there any evidence that the enrichment pupils were working as part of a positively interdependent group? What factors might make this difficult? How might Fatima frame Susy's difficulties as related to the effective utilization of cooperative group learning? What strategies might this suggest for dealing with what is then a problem of teaching and learning using groups?

Personal Reflections and Connections

1. Think about a situation in which you experienced learning difficulties similar to Susy's? How did you feel? In what ways were your difficulties affective? In what ways were they cognitive? What other important factors contributed to your difficulties? Explore other ways of framing your difficulties. What different strategies does each suggest? See if you can devise a strategy that takes into account more than one way of framing your difficulties?

2. Think of a teaching situation in which you were confronted with a pupil having difficulties like Susy's. How did you deal with the situation? How did you feel? What did you do? Can you see your actions as rooted in one of the four perspectives on teaching and learning? Explore some of the alternative ways of acting suggested by framing your difficulties in terms of the other perspectives on teaching and learning.

Reflections on Learning-to-Teach

1. What does Fatima's critical teaching incident suggest to you about teaching and how best to think about it, and about learning-to-teach and how we engage in it?

2. Use the developmental perspective on professional growth from Chapter 2 to explore the suitability of Brenda Proser giving Fatima the Enrichment Group. What effect might the continued presence of parents in Brenda's classroom have on how Fatima experiences this assignment? What prior experiences might have helped her work with the enrichment pupils?

MANAGING DILEMMAS: EXPLORING ALTERNATIVE WAYS OF TEACHING AND LEARNING

She sat alone, as the winter darkness began to fill her small apartment. Over a quiet cup of coffee after supper, Marina finally had time to reflect on the day's disaster and the previous week's math classes. She had established learning centres in the style suggested by her math professor, and the students had certainly enjoyed the activities and appeared to be learning their math. Today, however, when she presented them with a formal worksheet on the topic, it was as though most of the children had learned nothing. They had performed abysmally.

What was wrong? Marina had always hated mathematics and was determined never to teach it in the same boring manner she remembered from her own schooling. Then again, at least she had learned enough to be successful—something her grade five students had failed to do. Were the teachers in the staff room correct when they remarked that many of the innovative ideas introduced at the faculty were out of touch with the reality of today's classrooms? At the faculty, the ideas had made sense to her, and she was beginning to understand some fundamental math concepts. Did the children really need all the drill and practice she remembers with such distaste? She knew her cooperating teacher was concerned about the upcoming system-wide math test. Although he had given her the freedom to try some of her own ideas, she could detect that he was extremely anxious about today's fiasco. "How do children really learn, and what is the best way for me to teach?" she wondered.

INTRODUCTION

When student teachers enter a faculty of education, they may be confronted with a different vision of teaching and learning from the view they retained from their own schooling. During practicums, these student teachers might well be exposed to yet other notions of teaching and learning. Their student teaching experiences may or may not match their own or the new concepts discussed at the faculty. The experiences will, likely, be somewhere on the continuum between their memories and the visions of the future. This lack of consistency often surprises student teachers. They do not expect to find contradictions and opposing views. Rather, they anticipate close accord between their professors' and cooperating teachers' views of teaching and learning and their own. Student teachers, therefore, may be discomfited in the variance between these visions of the future and memories of the past.

What is it then that student teachers need to learn during teacher education, and how should that content be taught? Practitioners, whether they be teachers, lawyers, physicians or engineers tend to seek "detailed particulars that speak to their situation; they want an action plan, advice on what will work, and evidence that the plan will solve their practical problems" (Cuban, 1992, p. 5). Academics, on the other hand, are sceptical of blueprints or prescriptions, which offer solutions for solving educational problems (Marshall & Barritt, 1990). Professors want their student teachers to explore alternative ways of teaching and learning through several critical lenses, and to experiment with a variety of pedagogical practices. At the same time, student teachers must be aware that pupils in classrooms need to be protected from teaching strategies detrimental to their overall well-being. As Fullan (1982, p. 18) has indicated, change can be inspired by opportunism and personal gain based on faulty and overly abstract theories not relatable to practice.

Student teachers may find themselves caught in what Katz and Raths (1992) have called the "current practice versus innovative practice" dilemma. They may want to, or feel obligated to, attempt to use innovative teaching strategies. Student teachers also want to receive a good report from their cooperating teachers, and realize that one approach for achieving this is to maintain the classroom status quo. Attempting to satisfy diverse authorities while also trying to develop a personal philosophical framework for teaching and learning is difficult and may seem overwhelming to the student teacher.

Student teachers' histories and experiences also create dissonance. Most student teachers have been very successful as pupils in the environment to which they return as teachers. Why would they want to critically explore or change a process they perceived was good? For some, becoming socialized into the status quo is both comfortable and safe. On the other hand, others may have been frustrated with a certain style of teaching, or teacher. These student teachers may then be determined to change the system, no matter what, and may be unwilling to explore the wisdom and methodologies of established practices. Additionally, critical reflection on one's practice is difficult and may inhibit new teachers from exploring different strategies. It is a demanding and daunting task for the neophyte teacher who is attempting to cope with many new experiences. Survival, rather than change, often becomes the priority.

Helping student teachers explore alternative ways of teaching and learning might best be accomplished if teacher educators (in faculties and schools) view some aspects of learning about teaching as a series of dilemmas to be managed rather than as a collection of problems to be solved. In this chapter, we define the term *dilemma*, explore how the notion of managing dilemmas can be beneficial, and probe the current practice versus innovative practice dilemma. Using dilemma management removes the necessity of having to consider problematic situations as predicaments that have to be either resolved or left unresolved. Much of teaching is *messy*, and as such is full of dilemmas that cannot be resolved. Through dilemma management, educators are provided with another means for contending with the multifaceted world of teaching. In many ways, this chapter, along with the previous one on reflective practice, sets the stage for dealing with the case studies that follow, so we urge you to carefully consider the discussions as a means for effectively learning about teaching.

MANAGING DILEMMAS

In the course of a school day, teachers are expected to make hundreds of decisions, and people who are faced with problematic situations often have to make difficult, unattractive choices. Such situations can be framed as problems or dilemmas. A problem can be understood as a situation for which solutions can be found. Dilemmas, on the other hand, cannot be satisfactorily resolved. Lilian Katz and James Raths (1992) used the *Dictionary of Confusing Words and Meanings* (Room, 1985) to define the term *dilemma* as a predicament having two mains features:

> (a) It involves a situation that offers a choice between at least two courses of action, each of which is problematic, and (b) it concerns a predicament in which the choice of one of the courses of action sacrifices the advantages that might accrue if the alternative were chosen (Katz and Raths, 1992, p. 376).

One important question for educators to ask themselves is "How do I handle a dilemma?" Magdalene Lampert describes dilemma management as "a way to manage my dilemma without exacerbating the conflicts that underlay it" (1985, p. 183). Lampert suggests that on many occasions teachers cannot resolve the problematic situations. Instead, they have to *manage* these messy situations. They have to find "a temporary respite that [will] prevent the underlying conflicts from erupting into more serious, distracting discord" (1985, p. 185).

Lampert provides an example which occurred in her own classroom—that of maintaining control (by being in close proximity to the boys who sat together) while not excluding the girls from involvement in the mathematical discussions. Lampert's grade 4, 5 and 6 classroom had chalkboards on opposite sides of the room. The girls chose to sit together in a large group near one, while the boys congregated on the other side of the room. Neither girls nor boys wanted to sit next to a member of the opposite sex—a common occurrence at these grade levels. The boys were enthusiastic about their mathematics classes but also rambunctious, tending to tell loud silly jokes and behave inappropriately with the manipulative materials. The girls, on the other hand, were well behaved. Because of the different behaviour patterns, Lampert chose to write on the chalkboard nearest to the boys. This close proximity to the boys allowed her to maintain order in her classroom with a minimum of overt control. However, it also isolated the girls so they did not receive as much of her attention. One of the girls complained that she felt she was being ignored.

Lampert believed she had to make a decision based on two undesirable options. If she continued working at the chalkboard nearest to the boys, she could not pay equal attention to the more well-behaved girls. If she worked at the chalkboard nearest to the girls, she would not have the physical proximity for expediently quelling minor disturbances. Neither alternative was satisfactory, however, these were the two from which Lampert felt she had to make her decision.[1] She also realized that doing nothing was an unsatisfactory alternative. Lampert explains how it was important for her to be able to act with integrity while at the same time providing for contradictory concerns:

> I did not want to be a person who treated girls unequally as my high school trigonometry teacher had done. Nor did I want to be someone who gave special attention to girls just because

they were girls. I did not want to be a person who had such a preoccupation with order that I discouraged enthusiasm. Nor did I want to try to do my work in a disorderly classroom (Lampert, 1985, p. 184).

In her paper, Lampert discusses how she pursued a series of "losing arguments" with herself as she considered the merits and limitations of her various alternatives. Critical reflections of this nature, although heart wrenching and time-consuming, assist teachers in understanding the complex world of their classrooms. Instead of ignoring aspects of a situation that might contradict one another, managing a dilemma acknowledges the contradictions, accepts the conflict that arises, and searches for strategies that will support successful classroom practices.

Lampert realized that she was unable to resolve her problem. However, she did find a tolerable means of managing this dilemma that also let her meet another need. During this period, Lampert had a student teacher and wanted the student teacher to take on greater teaching responsibility. She therefore asked the student to team-teach. Lampert divided her class into four groups (two of girls and two of boys) with each teacher being responsible for one group of boys and one group of girls. These smaller groups allowed both Lampert and her student teacher to maintain order among a smaller group of boys, while providing more opportunities for the girls to participate and receive the attention they deserved.

It should be emphasized that the way Lampert managed her dilemma is similar to the way most dilemmas have to be managed. The course of action is seldom one that is permanent or generalizable, or even ideal. Dilemma management, however, does provide a way for a teacher to endure the dilemma over a transitory period. As we noted, problematic situations can be framed as problems or dilemmas (see Figure 4.1). Problems are *orderly* situations for which solutions can be found. Dilemmas, on the other hand, often occur in *messy* situations. They cannot be satisfactorily resolved, create further complications when left unresolved, and so have to be managed. Larry Cuban suggests that educational dilemmas often resemble problems in that conflict is present in both. Educational dilemmas, however, are "far messier, less structured and often intractable to routine solutions" (Cuban, 1992, p. 6). Under such circumstances, educators usually have to make difficult, unattractive choices since standard technical solutions are unavailable.

EXPLORING ALTERNATIVE WAYS OF TEACHING AND LEARNING

How can dilemma management theory assist student teachers and teacher educators? When student teachers enter university classrooms, they are sometimes confronted with new and challenging ideas concerning the process of teaching and learning. These ideas can be in conflict with those to which the student teachers were exposed during their own schooling, and/or in conflict to those they may encounter in classrooms during the practicum. Katz and Raths have called this the "emphasis on current practice versus innovative practice dilemma" (1992, p. 381). They point out that

> . . . a teacher education program faculty can choose to focus on helping candidates acquire competence in the current standard practices of the schools available to them or program faculty may give priority to helping candidates learn the most recently developed innovative practices— ones that are rarely seen in today's schools (Katz & Raths, 1992, p. 382).

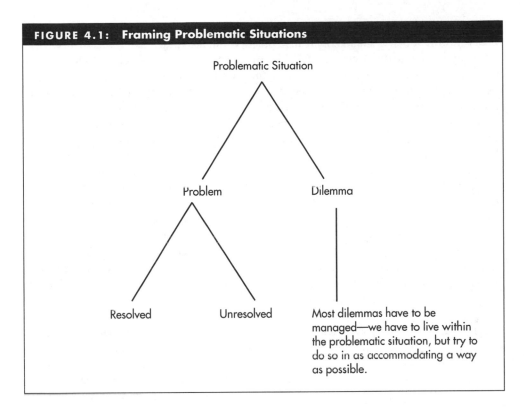

FIGURE 4.1: **Framing Problematic Situations**

Goodlad (1990) encourages teacher education institutions to help student teachers to learn innovative practices that will move education forward, while at the same time preparing them for the realities of classrooms. However, education faculties only have a finite amount of time and cannot adequately embrace all of the pedagogical strategies that should be included in the *ideal* program.

The conflict associated with the current practice versus innovative practice dilemma has often prevented meaningful dialogue between teacher educators at the university and teacher educators in the field (cooperating teachers), and has interfered with the education and training of student teachers. Cooperating teachers occasionally accuse faculty of not being in the *trenches* and, therefore, out of touch. Faculty, on the other hand, view some teachers as reluctant to adopt innovative teaching strategies. Since even under ideal circumstances communication is difficult (see Chapter 7), the two groups of educators need to work at the process. If the participants fail to respect the position of the other collaborators, an impenetrable obstacle can be created.

Acknowledging this conflict as a dilemma to be managed might well provide the time for both teachers and professors to recognize the strengths and limitations of each other's position. As Lampert states, dilemma management "requires admitting some essential limitations on our control over human problems. It suggests that some conflicts cannot be resolved and that the challenge is to find ways to keep them from erupting into more disruptive confrontations" (Lampert, 1985, p. 193). Respecting one another's position and complementing each other's competencies with student teachers has the potential to strengthen the partnership between teacher educators. Our new teachers have to realize that not only does theory inform both current and innovative practice, but also practice informs theory.

Many student teachers entering faculties of education consider teaching to be a simple process (Calderhead, 1987). Few anticipate the multifaceted challenges they encounter in today's classrooms. In mathematics education classes, for example, prospective elementary teachers often have to re-learn mathematical content as well as pedagogical processes. Many begin to understand the meaning underlying their rote-learned algorithms for the first time. As one student teacher explained (tongue-in-cheek), when discussing the algorithm for the division of fractions, "Ours was not to reason why, just invert and multiply." Uncovering the mystery of mathematics and other content areas, is both an exciting and intimidating prospect for student teachers—exciting, because they are learning material they never before understood; intimidating, because they realize that teaching is far more complex than they had anticipated.

Framing and reframing can help student teachers survive the failures and frustrations that are a part of developing their individual teaching styles. If student teachers are to be successful, they must explore alternative ways of teaching and learning, and be able to "frame and reframe the dilemmas encountered in teaching." (Harrington, Quinn-Leering, & Hodson, 1996). Teachers each have individual talents and diverse capabilities, so no one style of teaching will ever meet the requirements of all student teachers. During their university courses and practicums, student teachers need time to ask questions about teaching, and must be provided with opportunities to frame and reframe experiential situations. Realizing that there are many occasions to use more than one lens for viewing such circumstances provides student teachers with a repertoire of skills to manage a variety of situations.

Student teachers also want to establish their own identities, so they need a means for handling the inevitable stalemates between tradition and change which will often confront them. As Britzman wrote, "when student teachers step into the teacher's role they are confronted not only with the traditions associated with those of past teachers and those of past and present classroom lives, but with the personal desire to carve out one's own territory, develop one's own style, and make a difference in the education of students" (1991, p. 19).

Learning to examine a variety of teaching styles from a critical perspective helps student teachers tackle the difficult task of thinking about teaching, something most of us do only when we are truly in a quandary. Together, teacher educators must search for ways to challenge and engage student teachers so they consider alternative pedagogical strategies. Realizing that not all problematic situations have to be resolved, but rather that some can be managed, can assist student teachers and teacher educators. Certainly, not all of teaching is dilemma management; many are problems which can be resolved. However, student teachers and teacher educators should not feel inadequate when they encounter a complex problem that appears unresolvable. "These so called 'problems' are complex, untidy and insoluble. They are, I argue, dilemmas" (Cuban, 1992, p. 6).

We have described what a dilemma is, discussed dilemma management, and considered the use of dilemma management in the messy, problematic world of teacher education. You will now be asked to practice framing and reframing a problematic situation, and to explore the utility of framing the situation as a dilemma. The following two cases explore problematic situations faced by Marina, the student teacher you met at the beginning of this chapter, and her faculty advisor.

Exploring Alternative Ways of Teaching and Learning: Marina's Dilemma

Just when I thought the day couldn't get any worse, the door of the grade five portable opened and in walked Professor Alexander. I had just dismissed the class five minutes earlier, after what I thought was a disastrous math lesson and was discussing the situation with Mr. Shah, my cooperating teacher. The children just hadn't got it! All that work at centres on measurement, and when they had to do a worksheet on metric conversion, hardly anyone could answer the questions. I want to be a good teacher; I want the children to understand and like mathematics. Now the person who had encouraged me to teach mathematics using manipulatives at activity centres (a strategy that now seemed like a complete failure) was walking through the door. Emotions were high! Was I the failure or was he? Can pupils learn from each other, and do these *ivory tower* ideas work in the real world, or should we just teach in the boring old way that I remembered being taught?

I'm a fairly confident twenty-four-year-old who has just completed an honours degree in psychology. I decided, after a year in the work force, that I really wanted to be a teacher, so I enrolled in a one-year teacher education program, specializing in the primary/junior years (kindergarten to grade 6). One of the subjects I dreaded teaching was math. Although I completed calculus in high school and several statistics courses at university, I have always hated math. It always makes me feel anxious. All I can remember is math being drilled into me—

like it was for a test and no other reason. No matter what, I was determined never to put my students through the agony I had been through. I hadn't looked forward to my math education classes at the faculty, but after several weeks, my views about mathematics were changed. Professor Alexander actually made mathematics interesting, and for the first time in my life, I was beginning to understand concepts that had eluded me for years. I now knew how I was going to teach mathematics. My students were going to understand mathematical concepts and be able to apply their learning to everyday situations—not just have to memorize senseless rules.

But what happened? I set up measurement centres just as we had done at the faculty. I spent hours making the materials and activity cards so that they were interesting and challenging. The children measured objects using metres and then again in decimetres, centimetres and millimetres. Most of the students seemed to be developing an understanding of conversion. One pupil even asked me if she really needed to measure the object a second time because once she had measured it in the larger unit she knew what it was in the smaller unit. I was pleased with the way the learning centres were going.

I was sure the students were ready to move on to more abstract work with metric conversion, so I developed a worksheet for them. After starting it, almost all of the pupils raised their hands and said, "I don't get it!" The class deteriorated from there.

Now Professor Alexander was in the room and I was going to tell him that these methods just don't work. Tomorrow, I'm thinking of going back to the memorization of rules. It might not be as much fun, but the children will probably learn it more quickly and then might be able to pass the system-wide test that seems to be worrying Mr. Shah, my cooperating teacher.

I'm not even sure why I decided to teach this way. I mean, I learned math, didn't I? I got through university and I'm OK. What's more, I've been reading that many parents don't approve of this new way of teaching math and want us to go back to the basics. I guess I just heard that this is the way we should be teaching, and heard it, and heard it. Like, it wasn't just in math; I heard it in English, in science, everywhere. You know, now everything is supposed to be child-centred and active and based on manipulation of concrete materials. . . . So, I just thought, "Well, this is the way it is now."

But, maybe it is and maybe it isn't. I just don't know!

Did I really learn math? I certainly didn't understand several of the concepts Professor Alexander presented in class. I didn't know why six divided by zero was "undefined," or why fractions were inverted when you divide. When Professor Alexander said that one of his student teachers told him, "Ours was not to reason why, just invert and multiply," I thought, "Yep, that's me!" I knew the rules, but didn't understand them. Do I teach my pupils the rules so they just memorize them as I did and end up hating math? Or, do I try to teach them to understand, knowing they might not learn the rules? The next year's teacher will not be impressed, the pupils might fail the system-wide tests, and then I will have to answer to the principal and the parents, never mind the children. Teaching wasn't supposed to be this tough!

Exploring Alternative Ways of Teaching and Learning: Professor Alexander's Dilemma

As I walked into the portable, I saw disappointment all over Marina's face. She was putting on a brave front as she talked to Mr. Shah, her cooperating teacher, but it was evident today had not been one of her better student teaching days. What could have happened? Marina was one of the more competent teachers to whom I taught math pedagogy. She was intelligent, industrious, and keen to learn about the conceptual obstacles that hinder pupil's mathematical understanding, and to grasp the strategies teachers can employ to facilitate the learning of mathematics.

Marina explained how she thought her math lessons had progressed well during the previous week. The children had been working at self-directed activity centres and had been involved in their learning. They had appeared to understand the mathematics they were learning, and to enjoy measuring using various metric units. In fact, during the pupils' time at the math centres, Marina indicated that some of them had intuitively grasped the notion of conversion of linear units. Today, however, when they returned to a more formal lesson on metric conversion, they had no idea of how to do the worksheet. Marina felt as though the past week had been a complete waste of time. She was devastated. She had planned the centres carefully and followed many suggestions from her math education textbook, which I had reinforced during classes at the faculty.

As she spoke to me, Marina's emotions changed from disappointment to anger and then to confusion. I considered Marina to be an excellent student teacher. She was interested in exploring alternative strategies for teaching math and asked good questions during class discussions. I was quite certain that if anyone at the faculty had understood what I was attempting to teach about mathematics education, it would have been Marina. How must my other student teachers be coping if she was having difficulty? Marina was angry, disappointed, and frustrated. As I drove back to the faculty, I was also disappointed, frustrated, and concerned. My disappointment and frustration stemmed from the fact that I believe in a constructivist approach to learning mathematics.[2] One cannot drill conceptual understanding into pupils' heads. Pupils, especially young pupils, need time to manipulate concrete objects, discuss new ideas with their teacher and other pupils, and develop their own correct understanding. My 20 years of teaching mathematics to children had convinced me of that, and I

believe the strategies are the most appropriate ones for helping my students become competent teachers. What is more, I am not the only one who thinks mathematics should be taught this way. The majority of math educators endorse the same approaches I advocate, although the public and some teachers in our schools have not always endorsed them.

I was also concerned. Was I setting up Marina and my other student teachers for failure? Was I preparing Marina adequately for her teaching during the practicum and over the next 30 years? If Mr. Shah didn't believe in a constructivist approach before and had doubts about these new methods from the faculty, then now he would be totally convinced that his traditional strategies for teaching math were more appropriate than the new ideas. It had not only been a bad day for Marina; it was also a bad one for me.

The following morning, I revisited this dilemma. Why should my student teachers necessarily understand how to help their pupils make connections between abstract mathematical symbols and the concrete learning experiences provided by activity centres? A teaching experience, which had occurred some 20 years earlier, provided me with a vivid example of Marina's predicament. I remembered being introduced to the base ten materials during my early teaching years and thinking they would solve many of the difficulties my young pupils had been having understanding the regrouping process associated with addition and subtraction. My grade 3 pupils were very happy and successful adding and subtracting with the base ten materials, yet performed abysmally when they moved to paper-and-pencil calculations. At the time I thought I had a poor class.

Only later did I realize that my pupils had an inexperienced teacher who had failed to recognize the importance of transforming his knowledge to assist the pupils' understanding. I had assumed the transition from materials to pencil-and-paper calculations to be a relatively simple step. The pupils, of course, had been performing two quite discrete acts (one with the materials, the other with pencil-and-paper) and did not recognize the connection between the two.

Had I, 20 years later, missed a similar connection in my university teaching? Had I spent too little time helping student teachers understand the importance of making connections between the concrete representations for the mathematics and their symbolic forms? In fact, had I simply expected my student teachers to make many of these connections for themselves? After all, my student teachers only have a 25-hour course to understand all that is important in teaching mathematics from kindergarten to grade 6. Did Mr. Shah, understand the importance of making connections between abstractions and concrete representations? I spend very little time talking with my cooperating teachers about what I do at the faculty—and why I do it. There certainly seems to be little connection between faculty course work and the practicum. How wide is the theory/practice gap really? And, can it be narrowed? As I considered these dilemmas, the phone rang. It was Marina.

QUESTIONS

Framing, Reframing, and Exploring Solutions

1. Frame the case from
   i)   Mr. Shah's perspective
   ii) Marina's perspective
   iii) Professor Alexander's perspective

2. For each person, decide if the situation was a dilemma or a problem. What information did you use to make your decision?

3. How could each person either manage the dilemma or solve the problem?

Personal Reflections and Connections

1. Recall any experience you have had that was similar to Marina's. How did you handle the situation and your post-teaching reflections? Would you now handle the situation differently? If so, reflect on some of the differences and discuss your rationale.

2. How can you help novice teachers understand teaching practices which you, or your student teachers, might never have experienced as pupils?

3. Provide examples from your own teaching experiences to illustrate the differences between a problem and a dilemma.

4. Professor Alexander saw Marina caught in the "current practice versus innovative practice" dilemma. Consider times when you have experienced this same predicament. What can be done to manage the dilemma?

Reflections on Learning-to-Teach

1. How is reflective practice linked to the managing of dilemmas?

2. How can teacher educators use dilemma management to help student teachers in their learning about teaching?

3. Marina knew immediately that her teaching strategy was not as effective as she would have liked, and upon further reflection, she became increasingly concerned. Identify ways in which Marina might have used the centre activities so that they would have assisted the children's understanding of conversion and enabled them to answer the worksheet questions correctly.

ENDNOTES

1. The reader should be aware that Lampert spent considerable time reflecting on other alternatives such as pairing the boys with the girls, or using desks instead of tables with everyone facing one of the chalkboards. She rejected these alternatives as unsatisfactory for her style of pedagogy in this particular teaching context. Each solution seemed to present further complications.

2. Constructivism is based on the theory that people construct knowledge for themselves rather than having others construct it for them. As Plutarch stated over two thousand years ago, "The mind is not a vessel to be filled but a fire to be kindled."

THE POLITICS OF TEACHING: ISSUES OF POWER AND AUTHORITY IN PROFESSIONAL CONTEXTS

Like it or not, establishing authority in the classroom and learning to use power well are two tasks student teachers must master to become effective. School memories of powerlessness in the face of injustice fix themselves vividly in our memories. Recall the time a teacher reprimanded you for talking when it was Sharma sitting behind you who had disrupted the class. Or think of the day your history assignment went missing although you knew you had handed it in on time. Such memories underscore the reality that teachers have considerable power to influence the course of events, while pupils have relatively little. The role of teacher places an individual *in authority* over other individuals (pupils). As a sociopolitical institution, the school provides a structure for evaluation of learning and control of behaviour within which teachers exercise *institutional authority*. Report cards, tests, formal structuring of time, defined norms of behaviour, all provide teachers with the power to exercise their institutional authority. Concern about "being seen as teachers," i.e., having pupils acknowledge their authority, is a significant issue for student teachers. How are they to cope with situations where pupils don't pay attention, won't stop talking, or refuse to do their homework? In a very real sense, the public display of an individual's competence to take on the role of teacher rests on his or her ability to be *in authority*—i.e., to successfully direct the behaviour of pupils in the classroom.

The student teacher's ability to assume the role of teacher, however, is not the only aspect of practice teaching where issues of power and authority intrude. At the same time as student teachers are attempting to come to grips with being in authority over students, they also face the reality that their cooperating teachers (and faculty advisors) are *in authority* over them. Cooperating teachers write those all-important Practice Teaching Reports, which to a considerable degree determine student teachers' job prospects after graduation, or even whether or not they get to graduate! These two authority relationships produce ambiguity and anxiety for student teachers. How they negotiate the sharing of authority—on the one hand with their cooperating teacher and on the other with pupils—will to a considerable degree shape the quality of their student teaching experience.

TWO KINDS OF AUTHORITY: POSITION AND EXPERTISE

In considering the process of taking on authority in the classroom, it is useful to distinguish between two types of authority (Peters, 1959). They are *authority of position* and *authority of expertise.* Authority of position arises from an individual's institutional or societal role (e.g., teacher, police officer, judge, prime minister). We obey the uniformed officer's directions to detour off the main highway not because we understand why this is necessary (in fact, the highway may look perfectly clear), but because his uniform identifies him as a police officer and society has granted him the authority to do this.

In contrast, we can submit to an individual's direction because we are aware that they have certain expertise. Our friend Chris makes fantastic bread. Its texture is always uniform and its flavour outstanding. We follow his directions about how to knead the bread dough, not because he is "prime minister of the kitchen," but because he is demonstrably *an authority* on baking bread. Our willingness to follow Chris's directions is based on his *authority of expertise* and our awareness of it.

Classroom teachers need to draw on both the authority of position and the authority of expertise. Initially learners, just because they are learners, are in a poor position to recognize a teacher's expertise. Submitting to a teacher's instruction involves trusting that the teacher can assist in learning a particular subject matter. Consequently, teachers have to rely on their authority of position to begin (and frequently to sustain) the instructional process.

Being In *Authority*: Looking Like a Teacher

Learning to manage authority involves understanding and displaying marks of authority. In a courtroom, we can identify the judge by her robes, behaviour, and the way in which lawyers, clerks, and security personnel behave towards her. Teachers do not have distinctive robes, however, similar markers identify them as being *in authority*. While the way teachers dress is not as distinctive as it used to be and varies from school to school, it is different from the way pupils dress. Most of the markers, however, are behavioural. Teachers stand at the front of the room; they move more freely about the room; they sound "authoritative"; they *take charge*. Most distinctively, however, they do what teachers do, i.e., ask questions, critique answers, direct behaviour. While it is important that a teacher be *in authority* in the classroom, we do not mean to suggest that a teacher's expertise is not also essential. The ideal is that a teacher be *an authority* who is *in authority*.

Establishing themselves as being *in authority* in the classroom is a vital step for student teachers. Complicating this task is the fact that a student teacher's experience as a learner has been very different from that of the majority of pupils whom they face. Typically, individuals who enter teaching have had successful and enjoyable school experiences. Coming from families who saw education as the central vehicle for self-advancement, they are prepared to submit to the authority of the teacher (at least in public), and in a variety of ways assume the role of *good student*. Yet, many pupils have not had such positive experiences. School, instead of being a fulfilling experience, has been a devaluing one that has confirmed their deviance and inferiority. Consequently, it is not surprising that some pupils rebel against the authority that the school and teacher represent. For most teachers developing an understanding of, empathy towards, and strategies for managing pupils who are rebellious *outsiders* is very demanding and frequently frustrating. However, ongoing negotiation with pupils regarding the shared responsibility for learning is a central commitment of the professional teacher. The distinguishing mark of competence in this arena is the fair and judicious employment of the *power* that being *in authority* gives teachers.

Legitimate institutional authority carries with it *power* to influence those over whom one has authority. Teachers ask students questions, evaluate their answers, assign marks to their work, provide punishments for inappropriate behaviour, etc. In general, students submit to these actions because they acknowledge the authority of the teacher. They can, however, as every new teacher learns all too quickly, refuse to submit. When this occurs, the teacher may employ the power that goes along with the position. The teacher may assign a failing grade, send the student to the principal's office, or demand that an assignment be redone. There are limitations, however, to the use of such *direct power*. Its punitive character invariably provokes hostility and can even lead to open rebellion. One's ability to employ direct power is inevitably circumscribed by school policy, by administrators' predilections, and (most directly for student teachers) by one's cooperating teacher. Inevitably, pupils become knowledgeable about how a teacher's power is restricted and can effectively use this knowledge to advance their own diverse agendas in the classroom.

Being an *Authority*: The Multifaceted Nature of Teachers' Expertise

While it is an oversimplification, teachers' expertise is often broken down into two broad areas—subject matter and pedagogy. Typically, as a result of undergraduate study in a field, student teachers are relatively secure in their subject matter expertise. Pedagogical knowledge is usually seen as the focus of professional course work in teacher preparation, and practice teaching as the central arena for developing practical pedagogical expertise. So, while novice teachers feel confident that they know their subject matter, they are frequently not as confident about their ability to engage pupils in learning that subject matter. When student teaching exposes novices to pupils who have severe difficulties with material that appears relatively straightforward, they can experience acute anxiety. In the face of such crises, it is all too easy to revert to pedagogical strategies that emphasize teachers telling, and learners rote memorizing and executing routines. Such moves, however, result in increased reliance on student teachers' *authority of position* and decreased reliance on their *authority of expertise*. Pupils are being asked to follow the teacher's directions because the teacher *is the teacher*, rather than because they recognize that those directions facilitate their learning and enhance their lives. While such modes are, at times, unavoidable, excess reliance on them can be problematic for beginning teachers in the process of establishing that they are *in authority* in their cooperating teachers' classrooms.

Consider for a moment the problem of teaching pupils how to divide a whole number by a simple fraction. This process can be taught as the application of the rule: "Invert the fraction and multiply." A pupil involved in dividing 3 by 1/4 would invert the 1/4 to get 4/1 and calclate the product of 3x4/1 to get 12. Such a teaching strategy, on its own, requires that the pupil submit to the authority of the teacher, essentially to memorize the rule and carry out the procedure as directed. Such a strategy does not involve the demonstration of the teacher's subject matter expertise, i.e., her understanding that there are four quarters in each whole, and because we have three wholes (each with four quarters), we would have $(4 + 4 + 4)$, 12 quarters in total. Instruction that draws on the teacher's *authority of expertise* is aimed at developing pupils' understanding of what they are doing, not just so they know why there are 12 quarters in 3, but also so that they will be in a position to modify and extend this procedure to deal with different situations in the future.

Teaching methods rooted in the demonstration of a teacher's *authority of expertise* are undoubtedly more complex than is simple telling. From the constructivist perspective on learning introduced in Chapter 2, it is apparent that pupils generally have their own sets of preconceptions, i.e., they are not *blank slates* but already have ideas about what teachers are attempting to teach them. Pupils use these preconceptions when making sense of their teacher's instruction. When these preconceptions differ from those that the teacher has assumed, pupils may interpret instructions in ways very different from what the teacher may have intended. A pupil who has developed a view of *animals* as creatures, e.g., dogs, cats, cows, fundamentally inferior to people, will at the very least be mystified by his teacher's claim that "human beings are animals." After all, he is quite aware that when Suzi calls him "an animal," she is expressing outrage at his behaviour, not engaging in a literal description.

THE CHALLENGE OF BEING *IN AUTHORITY* IN SOMEONE ELSE'S CLASSROOM

For many student teachers, the most problematic aspect of student teaching is the obvious but frequently ignored fact that they are temporary visitors in someone else's classroom. Pupil rather than student teacher learning is the raison d'être of the classroom, and the cooperating teacher is the individual ultimately responsible for that pupil learning. In addition, pupils naturally establish a relationship with their teacher and to some extent the student teacher is intruding. Consequently, it is quite natural for pupils to turn to the cooperating teacher when conflict or confusion arises. How student teachers handle such situations makes a significant difference to their efforts to establish their own classroom authority.

In addition, student teachers enter a classroom in which the routines, norms of interaction, and networks of relationships have already been established. Consequently, initially they can focus fruitfully on observing these aspects of classroom culture to prepare themselves to work within it. Because deviating from classroom norms disrupts pupils, in order to succeed, student teachers need to carefully plan changes and to negotiate them with both the cooperating teacher and the pupils. The details of classroom expectations can serve as valuable discussion points for cooperating teacher/student teacher conferences. Student teachers' questions about the rationale for tacitly understood classroom norms and routines can assist cooperating teachers in articulating these important aspects of their practice. Such questions can also surface the world of dilemmas that emerges between professional ideals and practical constraints, dilemmas that are more frequently *managed* rather than resolved. Obviously, such open discussion does not come about easily. (We will explore communication in greater detail in Chapter 7.) On the one hand, it requires cooperating teachers to demonstrate that they are *an authority*; on the other hand, it requires novice teachers to—at least provisionally—accept cooperating teachers as being *in authority*.

Fundamental to fruitful discussion between cooperating teachers and novices is an awareness that they may well observe the same event based on very different conceptual understandings about teaching, learning, subject matter, and learning-to-teach. The importance of this point was vividly brought home to one of the authors in his first year as a faculty supervisor. John, a student teacher, was less than happy about his student teaching placement.

> As he explained it, he had been in Stan's biology classroom for almost a week and had not yet had an opportunity to *teach*. He was adamant that his placement had to be changed. After listening for a while, I inquired if the problem was that Stan was still doing all of the teaching. John's response took me by surprise. "No. He is not teaching either." Further conversation revealed that at the beginning of the week the class had been divided into groups to work on a series of group investigations. The results of these investigations were to be presented to the full class early in the following week. For most of the week Stan had been consulting with groups about their experimental designs, helping them assemble equipment, directing them to relevant references books, etc. (John apparently had been quite unsure about what he was to have been doing.) However, at no time during the week had anyone stood at the front of the class and delivered a lesson.

Needless to say, Stan saw himself as extremely busy teaching the class. John was just as certain, however, that "no *real* teaching had been going on." (It might be interesting to speculate about the compatibility of John's and Stan's viewpoints with the four perspectives on teaching presented in Chapter 2.)

CONTEXTS OF POWER AND AUTHORITY: FINDING ROOM TO NEGOTIATE

The pedagogical relationship between cooperating teacher and student teacher is fundamentally an unequal one, a factor that student teachers need to learn to deal with well. Most critical to a good outcome is the stance student teachers adopt in negotiating these relationships; the results can have significant consequences for their student teaching experience. As we see it, the stance adopted plays a major role in determining the quality of the professional learning that is possible.

On the one hand, it is quite clear that cooperating teachers are *in authority* with the power to make a significant impact on the career opportunities of student teachers. Student teaching reports written by cooperating teachers are probably the most important documents that a novice teacher brings to an employment interview. On the other hand, a student teaching experience, which involves replicating a cooperating teacher's practice is unlikely to facilitate either a broad understanding of the complexity of pedagogical practice, or the development of a student teacher's unique potential.

In the face of this dilemma, student teachers adopt a variety of coping strategies. All too frequently, however, they take an overly compliant approach, which seriously limits their own potential for growth. In our view, cooperating teachers and student teachers need to continually renegotiate their relationship to accommodate differences, professional growth, and the particulars of the teaching situation, ever mindful of the evaluative responsibility of the cooperating teacher. (We will return to this critical evaluation role and address the tensions it produces for cooperating teachers in Chapter 11.)

Goodman (1998), in a study of 10 reflective, elementary preservice teachers, has explicated five coping strategies adopted: *overt compliance, critical compliance, accom-*

modative resistance, resistant alteration, and *transformative action.* While these categories do not exhaust the possibilities, they do suggest a continuum of strategies for dealing with unequal power. In Figure 5.1, we have provided our interpretation of these five coping strategies.

Overt compliance would appear to represent an extreme stance, which seriously restricts student teachers' potential for growth during the practicum. Situations in which this coping strategy is adopted over any length of time appear to require serious remediation. *Critical compliance* overall would appear to be healthier, particularly for the initial stages of a placement. This cautious approach acknowledges a student teacher's vulnerability. However, during the later stages of the practicum when student and cooperating teacher have developed the necessary rapport and trust, both need to explore the potential of *accommodative resistance* and *resistant alteration.* Stances such as these are necessary if student teachers are to develop into competent, critically reflective professionals. In many ways, we see *transformative action* as the kind of stance that teachers strive for over the duration of their professional career. While it would be very difficult for a student teacher to achieve such a stance for a sustained period, as a professional goal, it serves an extremely important function for all of us.

FIGURE 5.1: Dealing with Power and Authority: Coping Strategies

Overt compliance
- student teacher suspends own beliefs; *adjusts thinking* to fit into classroom culture
- focuses on learning *how to* execute cooperating teacher's instructional procedures
- little concern with *what* is being taught or *why*

Critical compliance
- student teacher adopts existing instructional procedures but maintains an expectation that things will be different in *his/her own classroom*
- does not *adjust thinking* to that of existing classroom norms
- feels uncomfortable voicing criticisms of classroom practice; concerned about *alienating cooperating teacher* and getting a poor evaluation

Accommodative resistance
- student teacher adopts expected procedures in the main, but also develops activities that provide alternatives to regular classroom routine
- often sees these alternative activities as *making learning fun*

Resistant alteration
- student teacher focuses on making instruction *personally meaningful* for self and pupils
- attempts to provide *more substantive educational experiences* for pupils within the general expectations of the classroom curriculum
- employs alternative materials and activities that reflect different views of *what* should be taught and *why*

Transformative action
- student teacher focuses on meeting the educational needs of pupils by planning and implementing a unit of study around a personally relevant topic
- employs a wide variety of activities to facilitate the learning of diverse pupils
- engages pupils in *critical inquiry* that pays attention to *how knowledge is produced and justified*

These coping strategies provide a useful set of categories with the potential to increase understanding of the tensions inherent in the cooperating teacher/student teacher relationship. They suggest modifications to that relationship that could enhance student teacher learning. At the same time, they should not be thought of as providing a rigid prescription for how the cooperating teacher/student teacher relationship should develop. Human relationships are just too complex and multifarious to sustain such an interpretation.

Before concluding this section, we would like to deal with relationships that have gone very wrong. Any unequal power relationship offers the potential for exploitation, which may take many forms—from sexual and emotional abuse to excessive work demands. In general, student teachers have resources for dealing with such situations. Typically, these include university student service personnel, school administrators, and teacher federation representatives. Probably the first person to consult is the faculty advisor. What is important, however, is that student teachers be aware of the possibility of exploitation, of the resources to draw on if they suspect that they may be victims, and of their right and responsibility to take appropriate action.

Mei-Lin's Predicament: How Can I Be Seen as a *Real* Teacher?

Mei-Lin was in the fifth week of her practice teaching assignment at Parkview Secondary School. As she thought back over her first month, she realized that she had come a long way. Her honours biochemistry degree had certainly provided a comprehensive subject-matter background for working with both the grade 10 science and grade 11 chemistry classes. Doug Stinner, her cooperating teacher, was an older man. His hair showed touches of grey and the students seemed to think that he had been at Parkview forever. He wasn't particularly demonstrative or talkative with either staff or students. She found this rather disconcerting. Certainly it contrasted sharply with her own upfront manner and bubbling enthusiasm. Doug, however, was respected for both his years of experience and the high standards he set for his pupils. Over the last four weeks, she had come to appreciate that while he ran a very low-key class, the pupils certainly learned their chemistry.

It now seemed so obvious that her initial preoccupation with students liking both chemistry and herself had distracted her from the more central tasks of organizing, instructing, and monitoring learning. At the same time, her work with the girls' soccer team had helped her better understand adolescent learners. The fact that the soccer team had made it into the county finals helped her profile as well. Interestingly, she now found herself better able to appreciate Doug's first day injunction that classroom management needed to be the initial focus of learning-to-teach. At the time, she had been somewhat appalled.

This afternoon, Brad Anderson, her faculty supervisor, was going to observe her fourth period class. She felt quite good about the prospect. The grade 10s were lively but cooperative, and their study of the effects of the thermal expansion of metals had been going very well. Today, she would have them do an activity illustrating the expansion of three different liquids, and finish up with a neat demonstration of thermal expansion in gases. It should provide an excellent opportunity both to review what they had learned about solids and to extend this knowledge to liquids and gases.

The class went very well. She was a little apprehensive about both Doug and Professor Anderson observing at the same time. They really looked formidable, both rapidly scribbling notes at the back of the class. However, once she got the class going everything went very smoothly. Mei-Lin was very pleased that Professor Anderson had liked her demonstration. They had an excellent conference in the following period. It was really amazing how the same classroom event could be framed in so many different ways, and how different ways of seeing an event could lead to very different responses. Mei-Lin was quite excited about trying out some of the things that they had talked about. Perhaps cooperative groups could be used to provide more information about her students' different understandings? However, she wasn't quite sure what Doug would think of groups in his chemistry class.

This uncertainty had prompted her to press Professor Anderson again about the coolness of her relationship with Doug. She really felt quite uncomfortable. As she told Professor Anderson, there seemed to be "a distance between them," which she just hadn't been able to close. As she saw it, Doug didn't see her as "a real teacher . . . merely a student teacher." However, what brought things to a head for her was the incident in last week's chemistry class. In the middle of a discussion on the filling of the electron orbitals in atoms, Doug abruptly stood up and took over. Afterwards she realized that he must have been concerned

that pupils recognize the significance of the chemical properties of elements resulting from the number of electrons in their outer orbital. At the time, however, she couldn't imagine what he thought he was doing.

> When he finally stopped talking and sat down, I really didn't know what to do. The rest of my lesson was terrible. I just couldn't get going again. Afterwards, he didn't say anything about the lesson, but I knew I had fallen apart. Ever since that class, I don't really feel in charge. I'm continually looking over my shoulder . . . waiting for him to pop up and take over again.

Mei-Lin talked for quite a while with Professor Anderson. In fact, it was quite late when they left the school. While he was sympathetic and supportive, he also challenged her on some issues. He raised the possibility that Doug might not even have been aware of what he had done or its effect on her. He suggested that she needed to talk with Doug and see if they could work out some sort of mutually agreeable strategy for similar situations. It seemed to Mei-Lin that he was just making excuses for Doug. He even told her that she would encounter similar situations throughout her career, and that she had a professional responsibility not to avoid them but to deal with them. Mei-Lin seriously doubted if Professor Anderson really understood how vulnerable she was. After all, Doug would be writing her student teaching report, and she knew it was vital that he see her as completely competent. How could Professor Anderson really think that Doug would be sympathetic to someone who got upset over his taking over the class for a few minutes. He might even be insulted.

QUESTIONS

Framing, Reframing, and Exploring Solutions

1. This case has been written from Mei-Lin's viewpoint. Construct a plausible picture of the situation from Doug Stinner's point of view. How might Doug frame aspects of the situation differently? Why might Doug see things differently from Mei-Lin?

2. Mei-Lin's situation is complicated by her authority relationship with (i) Doug Stinner, and (ii) the pupils. How do you see each of these relationships? How does *power* enter into each of them? Explore how distinguishing between the *authority of position* and the *authority of expertise* makes a difference in how the situation is framed? To what extent are these two aspects of authority intertwined?

3. Use the five coping strategies to analyse
   (i) how Mei-Lin has been dealing with this situation
   (ii) Professor Anderson's suggestions

4. Explore how some of the ideas presented in chapters 1 to 4 might help you frame Mei-Lin's situation differently, e.g., Perspectives on Teaching/Learning (both for pupils learning subject matter and Mei-Lin learning about teaching), Professional Growth, Dilemma Management, etc.

5. In light of your analysis, devise a strategy for Mei-Lin to deal with the situation in which she finds herself. Provide a range of responses to deal with different possible reactions from Doug. Explicate a rationale for your strategy.

6. How might the policies and procedures of different institutional players impact and illuminate situations of this nature (e.g., school and school board, ministry of education, teacher federations and/or college of teachers, university practicum office).

Personal Reflections and Connections

1. Consider a situation in which you had to deal with issues of power and authority. Sketch out the details paying particular attention to what you perceived the problems to be *at the time* and how you dealt with them. After completing this analysis, explore how the situation could be re-analysed employing the conceptual structures presented in this chapter. What weaknesses and strengths does your analysis reveal about the use of these conceptual structures in making sense of such situations?

Reflections on Learning-to-Teach

1. This situation can be seen as rooted in a conflict between cooperating teachers' primary responsibility for the education of pupils and their responsibility for the education of novice teachers. As a cooperating teacher, what might you do to (i) try to prevent such situations from arising? and (ii) ameliorate the negative consequences of such situations when they do occur?

2. In this situation, Brad Anderson functioned in a counselling role for Mei-Lin. How else might he have dealt with the situation? What would be the advantages and disadvan-

tages of assuming different roles? What might Brad and the Faculty do in advance to assist both novice teachers and cooperating teachers in dealing with situations such as this one?

3. Unequal power relationships are the source of tensions and anxieties during the practicum. They can induce novice teachers to adopt coping strategies that seriously undermine their potential for professional growth in the short and long term. At the same time, they contain the potential for exploitation—both minor and extremely serious. What safeguards can be put in place to ensure that individuals in authority employ their power in an ethical and responsible manner?

A Demanding Practicum or a Case of Harassment?

Three weeks after finishing her four-week practice teaching placement at St. Olaf's School, Hannah had finally worked up the courage to see Professor George Papodopolous, her faculty supervisor. Since returning to the faculty, her anxiety over the experience had grown worse. Perhaps she didn't really want to be a teacher. In tears, Hannah laid out for George the litany of disasters that had comprised her four weeks at St. Olaf's.

From the beginning, Hannah had found her cooperating teacher, Bill Carson, extremely demanding and domineering. She was surprised to discover that he expected her to observe not only all of his classes but also a variety of other teachers' classes. For the first three days of her placement she had not even had time for a lunch break. On the fourth day when Bill found her taking a break in the teachers' room at recess, he commented that she would have to learn "to use her time more efficiently if she really wanted to be a teacher." She knew he was always first out on yard duty and would even work with some of the senior girls who wanted to improve their volleyball skills. However, she was quite exhausted after taking both the math and spelling lessons that morning. On Thursday morning when she walked into the staff room a little after 8:30, Bill remarked that she looked rather tired and suggested that she might be attempting to do too much. "Practice teaching is a full-time job," he quipped. When she reminded him that she had suffered from a chronic medical condition for more than a year, he looked somewhat pained. "Don't you think that you should get that cleared up before taking on a teaching job? Perhaps you need to see a new doctor."

In spite of her fears, the second week began very well. She had taken over one of the reading groups and it was progressing nicely. She had also presented the introductory lesson to the new unit on The Voyageurs. She was beginning to wonder if her problems of the first week had been primarily due to her inexperience. After all, she had had little to do with 11- and 12-year-old pupils. The boys, in particular, she found quite trying. Anyway, she was determined to start anew. By late Tuesday, however, she seemed to be back where she had been during the first week. Particularly annoying was Bill Carson's habit of referring to how she dressed. "That red outfit certainly caught all the children's attention today, didn't it!" Hannah liked to dress well, and she didn't see that it was any business of Bill's what she wore. On top of all this, she couldn't make much sense of his comments on her teaching. He seemed inconsistent and contradictory. One day he would praise her lesson, and then the next he would harshly criticize her "vague questioning" and "lack of classroom routines." As far as she could see she hadn't been doing anything differently.

At the end of the third week, Hannah had a particularly disastrous class. Afterwards she and Bill spent over an hour dissecting what had gone wrong. She knew that the class had not gone well, but Bill didn't seem to be able to find anything good to say about it. As their conference dragged on, she could feel herself wilting under his relentless criticism. What really unnerved her, however, was his very last comment. As he stood up to leave, he shook his head and sighed, "I know you can do much better Hannah, if you put the effort in."

The more she thought back over her experience at St. Olaf's, the more she realized just how controlling Bill Carson had been. He was always demanding to know where she had been—even during her prep periods. During her last week, he became quite angry, when she missed his last class to make a presentation to two other teachers' classes. (Ann Brown and Meeta Patel had been very interested in the research that she was doing on anorexia in adolescent girls and had asked her to give a short presentation to

their grade 8 girls.) Bill sounded hurt and accused her of finding other classes more important than his. She felt as if she couldn't make a move without asking his permission. It was more than the presentation incident though. She was always doing his photocopying, getting his coffee, cleaning up his room, or running an errand for him. She felt more like his personal gofer than a teacher. Teaching with Bill was nothing like what she had expected it would be.

Bill seemed to relish the power he held over her. He frequently reminded her of the report he had to write. "Don't forget about your practice teaching report. You are going to have to make improvements in your questioning and management skills for me to give you a satisfactory evaluation." Hannah felt trapped. She wanted to please Bill, but it seemed almost impossible. Deep down she couldn't imagine herself being the kind of teacher that Bill was. He was just so enthusiastic and seemed to have boundless energy. However, she figured that if she could stick it out for the four weeks—trying to do it Bill's way—she might make it. The last thing she wanted was a negative teaching report. Just before the end of the practicum, Bill suggested that they should write her summary report together. It was a total disaster. She didn't really know what he wanted, so she waited for him to take the lead. However, he must have expected more from her. After five minutes or so of uncomfortable skirmishes and awkward silences, she could tell that he was getting more and more upset. Finally, he wrote down, "Hannah has a pleasant nature . . ." and then stopped. With a sigh, he muttered something about not remembering student teaching being such a trial. He then closed his binder and left. The next day Bill handed Hannah her report and asked her to sign it. At the end of the day, he hurried off to coach the girl's volleyball team, so she really had no opportunity to discuss her report with him. She seriously doubted that Bill's report would be of much help to her in getting a job.

Professor Papodopolous was quite disturbed with Hannah's account of her experiences. He was particularly dismayed that she had not come to see him sooner.

He indicated that they would all have been in a better position to work things out if she had raised these concerns while still at St. Olaf's. After considerable deliberation, Hannah and George agreed that she should write a letter to Bill Carson outlining the events as she had experienced them and her view of their conflict. Professor Papodopolous would then set up a meeting with all three of them to see if they could resolve her concerns with the student teaching report and Bill Carson's behaviour.

QUESTIONS

Framing, Reframing, and Exploring Solutions

1. From Hannah's account, Bill Carson's behaviour was the major factor in her poor performance during the practicum. Construct a plausible account of what had gone on from Bill's perspective. How might he have seen the situation differently?

2. In retrospect, Bill did not appear to use his power as a cooperating teacher very judiciously. What aspects of the situation may have contributed to this? Does the *authority of position/authority of expertise* distinction provide any illumination of the situation?

3. What coping strategy did Hannah adopt? What were the advantages and disadvantages of this strategy? What potential might some of the other coping strategies have offered her?

4. Construct a plausible strategy for Hannah to employ in dealing with Bill on her own. Explicate a rationale for your suggestions, along with an analysis of the difficulties that a novice teacher such as Hannah would experience in carrying out such a strategy.

5. What external resources might be available for Hannah to draw on in this situation? How might she employ them? What reasons might there be for Hannah's apparent reluctance to call on them?

Personal Reflections and Connections

1. Recall any experience you have had that you suspect might have been harassment. What was your reaction at the time? What do you think your reaction would be today? Explicate the reasons for any change in your view.

2. Have you ever been accused of harassing someone—perhaps a kid sister? What were the ramifications? Explore how the concepts presented in this chapter might help you produce a more complex analysis of that situation.

Reflections on Learning-to-Teach

1. Situations such as those experienced by Hannah and Bill can be framed within a variety of different communities. What actions might members of these communities take to ameliorate the negative effects? Consider the response of the university practicum office, the university supervisor, methods instructors, the school board, the school principal, other teachers in the school, the local teacher federation representatives, and other student teachers.

2. Was this a case of harassment, or just a weak student in a demanding practicum? What actions might cooperating teachers take when they feel that a student teacher is particularly weak? How might they explore the possibility that they are part of a student teacher's problems? How might they attempt to ensure that student teachers get fair evaluations without compromising their responsibility to provide honest evaluations of prospective members of the teaching profession?

THE ROLES OF TEACHER EDUCATORS: COOPERATING TEACHERS AND FACULTY ADVISORS

The student teaching experience brings together three people: the student teacher, the cooperating teacher, and the faculty advisor. Frequently, each of these members of the *practicum triad* has very different expectations for his or her own role and the roles of the other two. In this chapter, we focus attention on the cooperating teacher, the faculty advisor, and the centrality of their relationship to a productive practicum experience for the student teacher. Considering the cooperating teacher and faculty advisor together reflects our view that both are teacher educators and that their productive collaboration is central to articulating a coherent teacher preparation program. We first consider their roles and working situations in an attempt to highlight the ambiguities and tensions that impede efforts to establish a collaborative and productive working relationship. We then consider two views of what is involved in learning-to-teach because they are often played out in the practice of teacher educators during the practicum. By making these views explicit, we provide the basis for a productive dialogue about the roles of cooperating teachers and faculty advisors as teacher educators. Finally, we provide a detailed look at three models of the coaching of teaching to provide teacher educators with a range of strategies for engaging novice teachers in learning from their experience.

CLARIFYING AND NEGOTIATING A COLLABORATIVE PARTNERSHIP

In some ways, the central problem of the practicum can be seen to be the clarification and negotiation of the respective roles of the three members of the practicum triad. In the last few years, a variety of studies have confirmed that student teachers, cooperating teachers, and faculty advisors have very different expectations. (e.g., Juliebo, Jackson, & Peterson, 1995; Guyton & McIntyre, 1990; Bandy & Alexander, 1988). While much of this book deals implicitly or explicitly with role expectations for student teachers, it is also important to deal explicitly with the roles of the teacher educators, and to explore ways in which differences in expectations can impede collaboration.

Typically, student teachers are assigned to a classroom to observe teaching practice, engage in teaching, respond to feedback about their teaching, and, more generally, become involved in professional discussions about teaching. Their cooperating teachers, however, are first and foremost classroom teachers, whose primary concern and responsibility is for the learning of their pupils. In general, cooperating teachers take on the task of guiding novices through their initial teaching experiences in addition to everything else they do, and with the unstated expectation that they can handle this task without impeding their pupils' learning. While school administrators may select individuals to be cooperating teachers, it is also common for teachers to volunteer. Typically they receive little or no training for this role and are forced to fall back on recollections of their own student teaching experiences. Given the hundreds of cooperating teachers required for even a small teacher preparation program, cooperating teachers find that their communication with the university is tenuous at best. Since they are more experienced teachers, they usually handle a variety of other school and board responsibilities. Being a cooperating teacher is also demanding. Cooperating teachers find that for the practicum period they become mentors, role models, counsellors, and evaluators of their student teachers.

In contrast with the roles of the student teacher and cooperating teacher, the role of the university-based faculty advisor is less clearly laid out. As Knowles and Cole (1994) point out, faculty advisors tend to be transients in schools. They come and go and seldom have any well-defined or ongoing responsibility other than to "work with" student and cooperating teachers (p. 190). Each teacher education institution sets its own expectations, but typically, considerable latitude exists for faculty to shape the role to fit their own strengths, preferences, and other responsibilities. Therefore, faculty members carry out their duties in a variety of ways, which can lead to confusion and misunderstandings on the part of cooperating teachers, student teachers, and faculty members themselves.

Left unexplored, such confusion can lead to feelings of wariness and distrust on the part of both cooperating teachers and faculty that seriously impede the establishment of a collaborative working relationship (Guyton & McIntyre, 1996). Unfortunately, perceptions of differences of status, both real and perceived, often impede efforts to resolve misunderstandings when they arise. The following anecdote recounted by Adkins (1999) illustrates how easily markers of status differences can intrude into the cooperating teacher/faculty advisor relationship.

During their first meeting, a group of cooperating teachers, faculty advisors, and student teachers decided to take a group photograph. One of the cooperating teachers suggested an arrangement with the faculty advisors sitting on the desk tops and the cooperating and student teachers grouped around them. On later reflection, she recognized this grouping mirrored her view of the two distinct components of teacher preparation: first the university and the student teacher, and then the cooperating teacher and the student teacher (Adkins, 1999, p. 159). Only later, after serious tensions had surfaced between her and her student, did she see how problematic this strict separation could be.

> When I first encountered difficulty . . . , I said nothing. Somehow, I was, if not threatened and intimidated by the university professors, under the misconception that I was inferior to them. . . . I was convinced that I had no place to voice my fears and to discuss my problems except with [the other teachers] (p. 159).

Needless to say, university faculty may hold similar views of the cooperating teacher/ faculty advisor relationships, views that seriously impede the open communication needed for the development of a productive working relationship.

Not only status differences, but also the very different work worlds of cooperating teachers and university faculty can lead to misunderstandings and confusion. Cooperating teachers are very much tied to the timetabling of the school day. University faculty, particularly when students are on practicum, have much more freedom to schedule their day. This does not mean, however, that university faculty are free to spend all of their time in schools. In reality, faculty members' teaching, including graduate, continuing education, preservice courses and practicum, constitutes about 40 percent of their workload. Research constitutes an equivalent portion, while committee work, through which much of the ongoing administration of a university is carried out, constitutes the rest. Given the steadily increasing teaching loads in universities (as in schools), it is not surprising that faculty members look upon the practicum as an opportunity to catch up on the research, writing, graduate supervision, and committee work that has been put aside during the preservice teaching term. While most faculty members carefully apportion their practicum time, there is little doubt that time management is an area of tension. In particular, it affects faculty members in their first five to seven years as they struggle to establish the quality research program required for them to move from probationary to tenured status.

A multitude of other contextual factors influence the growth of collaborative relationships between cooperating teachers and university faculty. However, fundamental to their mutual endeavour is their perspectives on the process of learning-to-teach of novice teachers.

VIEWS OF LEARNING-TO-TEACH

While cooperating teachers and faculty advisors hold a variety of conceptions of novice teachers' learning-to-teach, reviewing two extremes will help orient our discussion. One extreme is the *Sink-or-Swim*, or "You've got to learn to do it on your own" approach. This assumes that novice teachers have to learn how to teach by themselves, and that it is best for a teacher educator to provide emotional support, a classroom in which to teach, and then get out of the way. In its more moderate forms, it acknowledges the multiple differences among novice teachers and involves them in the task of constructing *their own style*. In its more extreme manifestations, it involves nothing more than leaving the novice with a class of students and telling them to get on with it. (Interestingly enough, this model predominates in the pedagogical training of most university professors.) Probably, it is the tacit nature of much of the pedagogical knowledge held by experienced teachers that accounts for the appeal of this approach, particularly among novice teacher educators. As is the case with many other endeavours, expertise in teaching is not sufficient for developing that expertise in novices. Faculty members and cooperating teachers often have to identify elements of their own expertise, of how they engage pupils' attention, monitor learning, and provide for individual learning needs, etc., before beginning to communicate with novices. Not only do they have to design pedagogical strategies that will assist novices in learning about teaching, they frequently have to construct the very language needed to explore what it is they do. In the absence of the ability to explicate their own expertise, it is not surprising that competent teachers frequently adopt a *sink or swim* view when first faced with engaging novice teachers in learning-to-teach.

In contrast, the *Do-As-I-Do* approach is based on a restricted behaviourist training view of how people learn-to-teach. In this approach, the role of the teacher educator is to model the required teaching behaviours and then, while the student practices these behaviours, to provide feedback that assists the student in modifying his or her performance so that it more closely matches that of the teacher educator. The primary focus is on the novice's imitation of the expert. Because of their expertise, teacher educators determine the particular lessons to be taught, activities to be used, assessment strategies to be employed, and levels of pupil performance to be required. Needless to say, this approach leaves little room for novice teachers to develop their own style. Instead, the focus is on the acquisition and refinement of *effective teaching strategies*. This view of learning-to-teach is firmly rooted in the skill development perspective on teaching and learning outlined in Chapter 2.

No doubt, we have overstated these two views and their differences. It may be difficult to imagine any teacher educator actually holding firmly to either extreme. More than likely individuals will combine aspects of both. Consequently, it is useful to represent these two views as opposite ends of a continuum of control as set out in Figure 6.1.

As soon as we move away from the *Sink-or-Swim* end of this continuum, we are faced with articulating how it is that teacher educators assist novice teachers. Essentially, this is the process of *coaching* typically employed in other contexts where novices learn to improve a performance, (e.g., in master's classes for musicians or artists, individual coaching for athletes, design classes for architects). What is typical of all of these learning situations is that a knowledgeable professional engages in assisting other professionals in crafting individual performances guided by broad criteria of what a good performance in the field looks like.

COACHING IN THE PRACTICUM

Effective coaching is a vital component of the practicum experience. In this section we will consider three different coaching models. The problems inherent in learning by experience during the practicum make demands on all participants. The central difficulty lies in the sets of conceptual categories that novices bring to learning-to-teach. Through these views of teaching, learning, subject matter, and schooling, novices *experience* both what happens in the classroom and the teacher educator's comments on what happens. When their categories

---

FIGURE 6.1: **Views of *Learning-To-Teach* on a Dimension of Control**

Sink-or-Swim _____ Do-As-I-Do

• must find one's own way	• mentor models and coaches
• learn to teach by teaching	• imitate expertise of mentor
• experience the "real" classroom	• take on "a bit at a time"
• develop a personal style	• develop effective skills

Novice Controls _____ Mentor Controls

are limited, or in other ways inadequate, novices experience teaching situations in ways that are unlikely to help them learn to perform competently. According to Donald Schön this aspect of learning by experience is the *central paradox of the practicum*, i.e., that novices at first cannot understand what it is that they have to learn, have to learn it by educating themselves, and can only learn by beginning to do what they do not yet understand (Schön, 1987, p. 93). Given this paradox, the way teacher educators coach novices is a prime determinant of what novices learn from their teaching experience. As coaches, teacher educators are concerned with how novices *see* (or frame) situations, as well as how they act in response to these situations. Using information gathered from pre- and post-teaching conferences and from direct observation of novices' teaching, teacher educators evaluate novices' pedagogical actions and their framings of situations. They then engage novices, through dialogue and action, in ways designed to assist them in exploring the consequences of different framings and actions in their teaching.

The interaction between coach and novice is delineated by three central characteristics: (i) it takes place in the context of the novice teacher's attempts to teach; (ii) it makes use of actions as well as words; and (iii) it depends on the reciprocal reflection-in-action of novice and coach. Schön (1987) has articulated three coaching models that provide alternative perspectives on the manner in which novice and coach engage in the learning-to-teach enterprise. These three models, *Follow Me*, *Joint Experimentation*, and *Hall of Mirrors*, provide a comprehensive view on the coaching role of the teacher educator in the practicum.

Coaching as *Follow Me*

In the *Follow Me* model of coaching, coach and novice achieve a significant portion of their communication through reciprocal actions. While the *Follow Me* model is rooted in the skill development perspective on teaching and learning of Chapter 2 and reflects the *Do-As-I-Do* pole of the learning-to-teach dimension of control, it is significantly complicated by the variety and complexity of the skills that make up the act of teaching. Typically, it is characterized by a three-part cycle. Initially, the teacher educator observes a novice's teaching, ascertaining what the novice already knows and what problems she or he needs to address. In light of this initial diagnosis, the coach designs an intervention, involving both showing and telling, with the potential to be meaningful to the novice and to result in a modification of his or her teaching behaviour. Finally, the coach reflects on the novice's reaction to the intervention, considering both talk and action, in an attempt to evaluate the accuracy of the initial diagnosis and the effectiveness of the intervention. Novices too engage in a three-part cycle. They attempt to decipher the talk and action of the coach, communicate their understandings by the manner in which they modify their teaching behaviour, and reflect on the consequences of their modified teaching behaviour.

In the hands of a skilled practitioner, this model of coaching will typically include a meta-commentary that articulates for the novice a variety of concerns regarding numerous decisions made by the practitioner on the fly. These include issues such as aspects of the context being attended to or ignored, and why; how actions took account of what had occurred yesterday, or last month, as well as what might occur tomorrow or next month; how actions supported or impeded long-term goals for the learning of the children; and other actions that were considered but not implemented, and why. Providing a meta-commentary while modelling teaching has been called *self-conscious narrative* after the literacy device used by novelists to direct attention to their own role in crafting a story. (For an extended illustration of a mathematics "methods" instructor employing this procedure, see Wood and Geddis, 1999.)

In contrast with the *Do-As-I-Do* pole of the learning-to-teach dimension of control, the *Follow Me* coaching model explicitly deals with the confusion, ambiguity, and inadequacy of communication between coach and novice that is an inevitable consequence of the central paradox of the practicum. However, the *Follow Me* model of coaching still leaves the control of the learning-to-teach process primarily in the hands of the teacher educator. As a consequence, it is likely more appropriate early on in the practicum, or in other situations where novices are unable to articulate with precision what they need to learn. The *Joint Experimentation* model, on the other hand, allows novices to assume some control over their own learning-to-teach.

Coaching as *Joint Experimentation*

When novices can be actively involved in diagnosing their own teaching, the *Joint Experimentation* model provides a style of coaching that gives them some direct control. In *Joint Experimentation,* coaches initially focus on assisting novices in formulating the qualities of the teaching that they would like to enact. While novices select an area of interest, their articulations are typically diffuse and not readily amenable to inquiry. It is the coach's role to assist in reframing the situation and in exploring potential solutions to the problems that emerge, all the while maintaining an ethos of *collaborative* inquiry. Frequently, this involves breaking down a more global pedagogical problem into a series of local problems that novices can engage in solving. The general problem of significant off-task behaviour occurring during a learning activity might be broken down into a number of parts: the teacher's initial explanation of the learning activity, the transition into groups required for the activity, monitoring pupils in the groups, and group (or individual) products to maintain pupils' accountability. As they explore possible solutions to the local problems, novices can choose those with the potential to yield the desired results. These choices can be made on the basis of how the strategies are represented in both talk and action during planning, or, in more extended inquiries, on the pupil behaviours that they engender. This coaching strategy engages novices in the critical activity of evaluating the effect of their teaching on their pupils' learning. *Joint Experimentation* provides novices with the potential to begin developing the *pedagogical inquiry* central to mastering their craft. For this to occur, however, coaches must firmly resist the temptation to usurp the novice's prerogatives to choose which problems to solve and potential strategies for solving them.

Both *Follow Me* and *Joint Experimentation* are strategies that focus primarily on the pedagogy that the novice is attempting to enact. Schön's third model of coaching expands the discussion to include the teacher educator's pedagogy of learning-to-teach.

Coaching as a *Hall of Mirrors*

Teacher education, unlike other fields of professional education, possesses a unique parallelism in that both novice teachers and teacher educators are *teaching*—the novice is teaching particular subject matter, and the teacher educator is teaching about teaching it. (This is not true in other fields. In medical education, for example, the educator *teaches* about diagnosing diseases, but the medical students *diagnose* them.) This parallelism in teacher education can lead to incongruous situations for novice teachers, in which the explicit messages of the content of instruction are contradicted by the implicit messages of the process employed. Such incongruity arises when novice teachers learn about the values of addressing "individual differences" or "active learning" in large group lectures, or when they are evaluated on their knowledge of multifaceted assessment strategies using multiple-choice tests. However, while this parallelism creates pitfalls for the unwary teacher educator, it also provides a resource the skilful coach can employ.

A coach using the *Hall of Mirrors* approach employs the learning-to-teach context in which novice teachers are immersed to illuminate problems in the learning context of the pupils in the classroom. The advantage is that it engages novice teachers in examing their own struggles in learning-to-teach for possible insights into the learning problems their pupils may face. Pupils' anxiety about getting the "right answer" may well be mirrored in novice teachers' anxiety about being able to answer pupils' questions. Exploring how their own feelings impede learning may provide novice teachers with greater understanding of their pupils' problems, and even lead them to design strategies to address the problems. At the same time, the *Hall of Mirrors* approach can help novices recognize how expert teachers deal with the complexity, uncertainty, and instability of classroom contexts. When coaches share their own uncertainties about framing classroom problems, designing strategies to help novices deal with them, or even deciding whether or not to raise specific issues, they make explicit the type of pedagogical inquiry in which they want novices to engage. Without doubt, there are dangers associated with these kinds of disclosures, particularly when a novice remains fixed on finding one magical recipe to solve his or her present problem, and is more than a little perturbed that the teacher educator does not provide it. However, using *Hall of Mirrors* has the potential to assist novices to move beyond the limitations of a purely technical approach to teaching. Likely, it is most appropriate to use in the later stages of the practicum, after novices have attained some competency in the basics of classroom management and direct teaching.

Schön's models of coaching provide three general approaches to coaching in the practicum. While superficially each might appear to be better matched to a different stage of professional growth, skilful coaches will find ways of creatively combining the three approaches to reinforce and supplement each other throughout the practicum.

There is little question that teacher preparation, particularly in the practicum, provides a substantive and ongoing challenge for teacher educators, both cooperating teachers and university faculty. On the one hand, the practicum is seen as the context in which everything comes together, where the real learning-to-teach occurs. Unfortunately, this view can engender in student teachers an increased perception of the irrelevance of theory (Rodriguez, 1993). It is not difficult to see how this alienation of practice from theory can occur if teacher educators approach learning-to-teach using the extreme *Sink-or-Swim*, or *Do-As-I-Do* modes. While we do not claim to be certain about the best way to guide novices so they appreciate the complexities of the classroom without rejecting the insight theoretical perspectives can provide, we are certain that achieving this goal will require a productive collaborative partnership between cooperating teachers and university faculty. Central to such a partnership is open and ongoing dialogue about the roles of all three members of the practicum triad and how they interact in the service of novice teachers learning-to-teach.

Exploring Two Sides of the Same Coin

Coping with a problematic student: A cooperating teacher's perspective

French teacher Marie Lavoie sighed wearily as she hung up the telephone after her call to Dr. George Miller, faculty advisor to Margaret Findle, her student teacher. Two days were left in this last practicum session, and she was exhausted and frustrated from working with Margaret over the last two and a half weeks. Marie' s call had been a desperate plea for help with Margaret's final teaching report. While Margaret was her third student teacher, none of the others had been as difficult. After talking with George Miller, she felt even more frustrated. Apparently, it was her responsibility to decide whether or not Margaret's report would be marked satisfactory or unsatisfactory.

Marie's concerns surfaced just a few days into their first week. Typically Margaret arrived shortly before class in the morning and was gone with the children at the end of the day. It was proving very difficult to schedule either pre- or post-teaching conferences to discuss her progress. Frequently Margaret would have either "forgotten" or "misplaced" her lesson plans for the day, and when she did have one to share with Marie it was sketchy and incomplete. In one case, she had written it on post-it notes! While she didn't want to be too uncompromising about the need for a lesson plan, Marie found it very difficult to focus on what Margaret's expected outcomes might be for a lesson. Even worse, the lessons were unfocused, leading to considerable classroom confusion. As the week progressed, Marie became more and more frustrated over the instructional time being wasted.

Margaret undoubtedly possessed an excellent knowledge of written and oral French. The pacing of her lessons, however, needed substantial improvement. Frequently, she spent the majority of the period reviewing. And while she used a variety of games, they were not always relevant or matched to the capabilities of the pupils. Her instructions tended to be muddled and incomplete. Consequently, pupils became frustrated and acted out. Typically, little time was left for the main topic of the lesson. While Margaret appeared to have spent considerable time and effort gathering teaching resources, she frequently was unable to use them effectively, either because of classroom management problems, or because she ran out of time.

Marie tried repeatedly to outline her concerns, but Margaret seemed oblivious to her hints and suggestions. She firmly rejected Marie's suggestion that detailed written feedback was important in improving teaching. "Actually, I prefer oral feedback," she responded. However, Marie did not find her any more receptive to oral feedback. For most of the first week, Marie struggled to engage Margaret in serious reflection. Their conference on Friday went relatively well. Together they outlined two major goals for Margaret's second week: (i) emphasizing planning and the articulation of lesson components, and (ii) getting better control of a variety of classroom management techniques. Just before they left the school, Margaret handed Marie a parcel, "A small gift to express my appreciation for all your help."

Marie arrived at school on Monday feeling confident that she and Margaret were finally on the right track. Just after the morning bell, Margaret came rushing in. She had had a "wonderful weekend visiting relatives in New York City" and had brought back a few "small souvenirs" for Marie and the pupils. As the day unfolded, Marie's sense of foreboding returned. Margaret's lessons displayed no sign of the approach agreed upon during Friday's discussion. Planning and organizational problems persisted, and class management was, if anything, worse. During one class, a child said to Marie, "Margaret doesn't care what we do, whether we work or not!" Marie tried to talk to Margaret over lunch hour, reminding her of the goals that they had set together. Margaret smiled while she cut out materials for the afternoon class.

As the week progressed, Marie found conferences with Margaret to be increasingly frustrating. Sometimes Margaret appeared receptive and commented on how much she was learning from Marie. Other times, she seemed quite antagonistic. At one point she blurted out something about Marie being so intimidated by Margaret who was 15 years her senior that she was hypercritical of Margaret's teaching. Pointedly, she commented that her previous cooperating teachers had not raised Marie's concerns. She even brought in her teaching reports. They were very positive.

Near the end of the second week, Margaret suggested that she would like to visit some other classrooms in order to experience a variety of pupils. Marie agreed and made arrangements with two of her colleagues. Unfortunately, they too had concerns with Margaret's lack

of control, unsuitable activities, and poor rapport with the students. They also confided that in the staff lounge they had overheard Margaret make negative comments about Marie's teaching.

On the Tuesday of the third week, the principal, Mr. Jones, dropped in to see Margaret teach. He too expressed concern about Margaret's classroom management and lesson organization. After talking with Marie, he suggested that she should contact Professor Miller. In the mean time, he encouraged Marie to keep the lines of communication open with Margaret and to continue searching for ways to help her. Hoping that somehow they could salvage Margaret's practicum, Marie developed a checklist of hints and tips for Margaret to keep in mind in planning and teaching lessons. Margaret seemed resentful and conveniently "misplaced" the checklist.

George Miller arrived just before lunch on Wednesday. He noted that there were only two days left in Margaret's placement, but suggested that they meet after school so that Marie and Margaret could share their perspectives on their situation. He would assume the role of a neutral facilitator, attempting to clarify issues and find areas of agreement.

Professor Miller suggested that Marie lead off. She began with the issue of the lesson plans being unavailable or on post-it notes. Margaret denied this, claiming that she always had full-page lesson plans, but that "Marie was too busy to look at them." Marie moved on to the lesson planning itself and her concerns with Margaret's selection of irrelevant and unsuitable activities. Margaret retorted that her lessons were well thought out and quite successful. In fact, she had spent many hours developing her own concrete materials because there were none available in Marie's classroom. She also noted that the children could have been a little disruptive because they were not used to so much stimulation and were unfamiliar with using concrete materials. The meeting continued in much the same manner. George Miller ended the meeting by suggesting that he would meet individually with Marie and Margaret the next day, after they all had some time to reflect on their conference.

On Thursday, Margaret's teaching was much the same. At lunch, she presented Marie with a bottle of perfume and a long letter of thanks. She chattered on about several games and eagerly jotted down the rules and variations of play for Marie. Dr. Miller arrived at the school in the afternoon to see if anything had been resolved. Marie wearily recounted the day's events. She felt anxious, but did her best to express her serious concerns about Margaret's lack of basic classroom skills. She really hoped that Professor Miller would help her with Margaret's evaluation. They talked at length about the anecdotal comments on the summative report and agreed that Marie should provide a candid and honest description of Margaret's work—her strengths and weaknesses. Marie, however, was still unsure of whether to assign Margaret a grade of satisfactory or unsatisfactory. Professor Miller wasn't much help. He insisted that the summative rating had to be her decision. He told her that he would call her the next day to see how she had worked it out.

Marie felt isolated and abandoned. She really felt that Margaret was an unsuitable candidate for teaching. At the same time, she did not feel that she should have to make this momentous decision about Margaret's competence on her own. She also wondered whether she would ever take a student teacher again.

Coping with a problematic student: The faculty advisor's perspective

George Miller was trying to complete the final revisions to an article that he wanted to submit to a very prestigious research journal. The courier would leave about 4:00, and he really wanted to get the article out today. If he was to move from a probationary to tenured appointment in the university, he needed a solid record of publications. When the telephone rang, he knew instinctively that it had something to do with one of his practicum students.

George was coming to the end of his first year at the faculty of education. It had been an exhilarating year. He loved his job, although he had had to move across the country and found himself working evenings and weekends to try and keep up. It was a relief to have some time for writing and research, though he enjoyed being a practicum advisor. As a former classroom teacher, he found it kept him in touch with schools, pupils, and learning. He had 12 practicum students in two schools and visited them weekly. He tried to meet with his cooperating teachers to discuss the students' progress, but frequently they were so busy that he hesitated to intrude. The students also seemed busy and involved. In some ways, he felt like an outsider. It wasn't that people were unreceptive; they just didn't seem to have time to talk.

The day before, George had been out to help mediate a problem at St. John's, but was fairly certain that the student and cooperating teacher could work it out on their own. Margaret Findle was a mature student teacher in her mid-forties, and Marie Lavoie, a young, relatively new cooperating teacher. Marie saw Margaret as so seriously disorganized that her lessons were unfocused and the children learned little. At times, Marie claimed, the children were "completely out of control." Margaret, in contrast, was quite effusive about her cooperating teacher and felt she was "learning a great deal in her classroom." She seemed relatively open to Marie's criticisms but saw the children's restlessness as resulting from her more innovative approaches, particularly the highly motivating and stimulating materials she had used recently for vocabulary building. All in all, Margaret was quite articulate about her teaching and its effect on the children's learning. She had confided to him, however, that Marie seemed a bit intimidated working with an "older" student teacher. She saw Marie as a rather "traditional teacher" who was somewhat overwhelmed by any noise or disruption in the classroom. However, she also acknowledged there was considerable room for improving her own teaching, and there was much that she could learn from Marie. George checked Margaret's records in the practicum office and found that her two previous cooperating teachers had rated her quite satisfactorily. In fact, one had invited Margaret back to help out in her class and was recommending her as an occasional teacher for the board. Neither Marie nor Margaret had invited George to observe Margaret's teaching.

As he picked up the telephone, George realized that he had not yet called either Margaret or Marie. He recognized Marie's voice. It was obvious that she was extremely upset and needed to talk. Things had not improved, and Marie was now faced with crafting her final evaluation. George tried to listen carefully and objectively. He asked Marie whether she might be slightly harsh in evaluating Margaret. Marie was quite annoyed and launched into an account of everything that she had tried to help Margaret improve. Finally, she got around to Margaret's evaluation and her quandary about whether or not to fail her. George took a deep breath and suggested that she should consider her decision very carefully. Obviously, Marie wanted George to tell her what to do, but it really wasn't his place to do so. He told her that she should complete the report as honestly and accurately as she could, and that the Faculty would support her decision.

George hung up feeling less than happy. He was quite dissatisfied about how he had handled the situation. He felt he had let Margaret down, and, at the same time, had failed to provide Marie with the support that she needed. As he looked up, he saw the courier pulling away, again without his paper.

QUESTIONS

Framing, Reframing, and Exploring Solutions

1. Drawing on the information available, try to infer how Marie and Margaret conceptualized what is involved in learning-to-teach. How might differences in their views have contributed to this situation? Might there also be differences in Marie's and Margaret's views of teaching French? How might these differences have contributed to their difficulties?

2. Can you infer anything about Professor Miller's view of learning-to-teach? How does he seem to see his role? The cooperating teacher's role? The manner in which they should collaborate?

3. The difficulties in cases such as this one are often framed as *problems in communication*. What factors seem to have affected communication between Marie and Margaret? How might these have been addressed? What about communication between Marie and Professor Miller? (Return to this case after studying the next chapter on Communication in Teacher Development. The concepts discussed there will provide a richer framework for considering the complexities of communication.)

4. Schön's three models of coaching provide broad perspectives on ways in which co-operating and student teachers might interact. Explore the potential of each for providing insights into how Marie and Margaret might have developed a more productive relationship. What resources, training, etc. might be needed to attempt to actualize these insights?

5. In Chapter 5, we articulated five coping strategies that student teachers use to deal with power and authority in the practicum. What was Margaret doing to cope? How effective was her coping? What other strategies or combinations of strategies might she have considered?

6. Faced with the diametrically opposed positions of Marie and Margaret, Professor Miller attempted to act as a facilitator to help them work out their differences. What other roles might he have assumed? How might alternative interventions on his part have helped resolve the situation?

Personal Reflections and Connections

1. Consider a situation you experienced in which a fundamental difference of perspective occurred on what was happening. Who was responsible? What factors contributed to the difference? What strategies did people use to try and work out a common response? What similarities were there between your situation and the one that Marie and Margaret found themselves in? Did a third party make any useful intervention? Should we always expect to be able to deal productively with such situations?

2. Think of a situation where you were in a position to mediate between two individuals. What did you do? Was it effective? What would you try if you were faced with the same situation again?

Reflections on Learning-to-Teach

1. What strategies might faculty advisors use to help improve communication with co-operating teachers in schools? What support do faculty advisors need to provide for cooperating teachers? How might teacher preparation institutions help faculty advisors provide support? (In considering these questions, try to keep in mind the constraints of time, money, and resources faced by both faculties and school boards.)

2. What strategies might cooperating teachers employ to improve communication with faculties of education? How might they negotiate the support they need to carry out the responsibilities they have been given?

3. Who should bear the primary responsibility for the final evaluation of a student teacher's competence? Present a detailed argument for your position.

COMMUNICATION IN TEACHER DEVELOPMENT

Learning-to-teach is a social endeavour and the ability to communicate is of paramount importance in this process. Communication is particularly important during the student teaching experience because typically so many people are involved. They include the student teacher, the cooperating teacher, the faculty advisor, student teaching peers, other members of the school staff and support personnel, the school administration, and of course, the pupils and their parents. Student teachers are expected to interact professionally with each person or group, and are evaluated subtly and overtly in each relationship. Generally, however, student teachers are concerned with organizing and planning suitable activities and with functioning successfully within their assigned classroom. They are often preoccupied with those tasks, and while they expect to receive evaluative comments from their teacher educators about their teaching, novices may be unaware of the importance of their own role in developing effective communication skills with supervisors and colleagues.

Open communication is at the heart of the honest and continuous feedback that student teachers require, and it is paramount if they are to further their understanding of teaching and learning. However, developing open lines of communication is often problematic, especially when student teachers are the ones who need the most information and feedback but have the least amount of expertise in teaching or communicating professionally. They are forced to depend on informed and reliable feedback from their cooperating teachers or faculty advisors in order to consider how they might improve their own teaching. Southall and King (1979) found that student teachers reported that their cooperating teachers' communication skills and feedback were two weak areas of support. Student teachers *want* constructive information because they are eager to analyse their teaching strengths and identify areas needing improvement. Student teachers also *require* such information because it is a prime means of learning-to-teach. Yet, most new cooperating teachers and faculty advisors have little, if any, training in effectively communicating their observations.

Few student teachers have had experiences that might assist them in communicating their questions or concerns to their supervisors. (You might refer back to Chapter 5 for a political discussion of this issue or ahead to Chapter 11 where we discuss the evaluation of student teaching.) Yet, learning, reflecting on, and practising alternative approaches which are likely to establish positive lines of communication are perhaps some of the most fundamental skills for cooperating teachers, faculty advisors, and student teachers to acquire. This chapter discusses the importance of the communication process and some of the impediments to communication, and offers suggestions and approaches which can help in overcoming communication barriers frequently encountered during the different phases of a student teacher's development.

THE IMPORTANCE OF THE COMMUNICATION PROCESS

Communication is an integral component in the supervision process of student teachers. Supervision, as defined by Acheson and Gall (1992), has three essential elements: (1) the planning conference, (2) observation and data collection, and (3) the feedback conference. Being able to communicate openly and effectively throughout each of these elements is vital if student teachers are to recognize their talents, hone their strengths, overcome weaknesses, and become reflective practitioners. It is crucial that the cooperating teacher, faculty advisor, and student teacher make open communication a priority. The tone established early in the relationship often determines the level of trust and safety student teachers experience. Barnes and Edwards (1984) found that the most effective cooperating teachers provided clear and specific feedback to student teachers. Nonetheless, developing a way to give effective feedback that makes sense and does not destroy the student teacher's confidence is challenging and only acquired over time, with effort on the part of both teacher educators and student teachers.

Likely, the most productive occasions for analysing teaching during the practicum occur during the one-on-one conferences between the student teacher and the cooperating teacher or between the student teacher and the faculty advisor after teaching occurs. Typically, conferences occur after the student teacher has taught but occasionally they occur after the cooperating teacher has taught and the two analyze the practices the experienced teacher used. During these post-teaching conferences, cooperating teachers, faculty, and student teachers find they have to recover and make explicit *how they do what they do, why they do what they do,* and *why they think the way they do.*

Addressing each of these features can be difficult for different reasons. Student teachers often find that surviving the day is an accomplishment. Until they understand the essential features described above, however, building on success and recognizing why strategies are useful or ineffective may be impossible. During these conferences, student teachers can reflect on their teaching experiences while sharing their concerns and expectations.

Teacher educators may find this process challenging as well. When considering why they do what they do, cooperating teachers and faculty advisors may have to revisit teaching strategies that, over the course of time, have become automatic. Under everyday conditions they no longer think about why they behave in a certain way or teach using a particular style. Cooperating teachers and faculty, however, must understand and be able to articulate their own practices before being able to assist others. Contradicting George Bernard Shaw, we would suggest that while those who *can* might *do*, it is those who know *why* who teach!

DIFFICULTIES IN THE COMMUNICATION PROCESS

The literature is replete with examples citing poor communication as a consistent problem in student teaching experiences (Southall & King, 1979; Guyton & McIntyre, 1990; Glickman & Bey, 1990). The problem may begin with poor communication and support for cooperating teachers from the university. "This lack of communication [can create] adversarial feelings toward the university and questioning of the expectations" (Koerner, 1992, p. 52). Cooperating teachers may not be aware of how they are expected to carry out their roles, which in turn, affects their relationship with their student teachers when they hesitate about the best way to proceed. The literature reveals that few cooperating teachers refer to theoretical frameworks or teaching innovations, tending to rely on their own practices and strategies, or falling back on the practices which they recall experiencing as student teachers (Ben-Peretz & Rumney, 1991; Koerner, 1992). Lack of familiarity with actual practicum expectations, or what expectations each person in the triad has of the other may inadvertently hinder the communication process.

As noted earlier, most communication between student teachers and teacher educators is in the form of feedback. However, there seems to be little consistency in either the type or amount of feedback student teachers receive. MacDonald (1993) reports in her study that some cooperating teachers either provided no feedback (a cause of great stress for the student teachers), or dispensed overly positive feedback, leading the novice teachers to question its validity. The student teachers "found that constructive criticism and discussions and analyses of teaching practices were rarely present during their practicum" (MacDonald, 1993, p. 413). In addition, most cooperating teachers tend to provide oral rather than written feedback on teaching. When student teachers have had a challenging day and are under stress, hearing, understanding, and remembering oral details can be problematic. Even when written feedback is provided, Wilkins-Carter (1997) found it to be "directed at 'fixing' a specific problem rather than providing feedback that encouraged thoughtful reflection about an underlying issue" (p. 242). This same study found most post-teaching conferences to be five minutes or less, hardly time for a two-way conversation or for any complexity to develop in the discussion. Providing feedback that involves and provokes student teachers, while not overwhelming them, is a challenge for even the most experienced teacher educator.

Conferences between teacher educators and student teachers tend to be uni-directional, with the cooperating teachers or faculty advisors leading the discussion and making the salient points. Their student teachers placidly try to interpret the advice being offered and what needs to be done to correct the situation immediately. Ben-Peretz and Rumney's study found that cooperating teachers viewed their student teachers "not as novice professionals but as 'students' whose primary duty is to listen and learn" (p. 525). In this study, the student teachers tended to be passive during conferences whereas the cooperating teacher was quite authoritative and prescriptive. Because student teachers and their cooperating teachers often interpret the same teaching incident in quite different ways, passivity further complicates communication. As adult learners, student teachers need to be encouraged to take responsibility for assuming an active role in the discussion, to ask questions for information and clarification, and to ensure they understand the information being conveyed. After all, these professional conversations are the most significant components of learning-to-teach for student teachers and occur only once during their professional career. The practicum is the only time when novice teachers have the benefit of ongoing, one-on-one support and advice from an expert teacher.

ASSISTING THE COMMUNICATION PROCESS

All members of the practicum triad need to work together to find ways to understand each other's perspectives and feel comfortable and safe discussing situations from another's viewpoint. Determining what student teachers expect to learn during the practicum, as well as discussing what is expected of them, are important parameters to establish early. In Chapter 3 we discussed framing and reframing. If teacher educators are to establish meaningful dialogue with their student teachers then they "need to have a rich understanding of the frames that novices bring to teaching" (Gonzalez & Carter, 1996, p. 46). They will then be in a position to view a situation through the eyes of a student teacher and begin to understand the preconceptions that novices often bring with them. Communication is enhanced when both parties are aware of the frame(s) the other is using. It is not possible for the novice to understand all of the frames of the expert. Consequently, the expert must attempt to interpret events through the student teachers' frames, while endeavouring to provide the student teachers with fresh insights on situations based upon their more varied experiences.

Cooperating teachers and faculty advisors have to communicate using a framework which their student teachers can understand. During the first few conferences, creating conditions that encourage student teachers to verbalize their preconceptions, and then listening to their beliefs, is probably more important than talking to them. Uncovering what novices understand, believe, and hope to achieve sets the groundwork for helping them move forward professionally. Similarly, student teachers have to consider why cooperating teachers and faculty advisors say what they do. It is too easy to accept or reject another person's position based on preconceived notions. Asking why and considering the response provide a starting point for understandings that can be accepted or rejected later, based on knowledge rather than ignorance or naivety. Considering and attempting alternative approaches under the watchful eye of an expert, then discussing the merits and limitations of the various strategies will assist the growth of the reflective practitioner. To promote reflective practice, communication needs to be focused on self-evaluation by the student teacher. Reflective teachers tend to be those who consider alternatives and the far-reaching consequences of their actions. Asking student teachers to consider why they do what they do, and guiding this reflective process, provides an approach student teachers can employ throughout their careers when reflecting on both success and failure.

While open and direct person-to-person communication is the most effective means to provide novice teachers with information, other methods not only support but also increase communication between novice and expert. Some are more effective than others for different people or for people in dissimilar contexts. The cooperating teacher might ask student teachers to keep a journal or log book with notes of themes that reoccur in their feedback and to look for possible explanations while forming personal goals. Such journals can help novice teachers verbalize and then discuss their analysis and possible courses of action. While some find keeping a journal is beneficial, others don't. In that case, video taping or audiotaping might be illuminating for some, though others will find it threatening. Some institutions are using a "bug-in-the-ear (BIE)" to provide feedback to student teachers during the practicum (Giebelhaus, 1994). These one-way communication transmitters offer the possibility for cooperating teachers to transmit short cues or advice to their student teachers or to provide online coaching in real time. Brief hints such as *give example, pause*, and *re-explain* are used to alert the student teacher that, in the teacher educator's opinion, the pupils are not understanding a particular aspect of the teaching episode. Student teachers reported that they were able to respond to the cooperating teacher's suggestions and that the BIE was especially useful when they were teaching a difficult or new concept to their pupils (Giebelhaus, 1994). Discovering how to communicate effectively is probably as important as knowing what to communicate. As teachers, we naturally consider the different learning styles of our pupils; we also need to remember that student teachers, cooperating teachers, and faculty advisors have different learning styles.

Discussing the day's events during post-teaching conferences provides worthwhile, prompt, and timely feedback, especially if participants are auditory learners. However, often a student teacher is tired or distracted by earlier events and does not *hear* what the expert teacher is saying during these conferences. Providing student teachers with written feedback highlighting key components that have been successful as well as aspects for them to consider in order to improve their practice (no more than three) is helpful. Student teachers can then reflect on this critique in the privacy of their own space. This thoughtful reflective time is likely to reinforce and strengthen the verbal communication of the post-teaching conference.

When observed data is provided—with actual quotes from the lesson whenever possible—student teachers are likely to accept the observations as legitimate and unbiased. Nonjudgemental evidence can be followed with questions for the student teacher to consider, such as, "What were your thoughts when Fatima said _____?" "Why did you do _____ in that way?" "When Brian has a problem, what does he do?" "Which pupils tend to stay on task when they are finding the work difficult, and who gives up easily? Why do you think they react in this manner?" Such questions help student teachers to reflect on strategies they have used effectively, and not simply dwell on aspects that need to be improved. Through subsequent discussions and/or written communication, student teachers need to be provided with opportunities to clarify their thought processes and preconceived notions pertaining to what constitutes successful teaching.

Student teachers, as adult learners, need to develop assertive communication skills and assume ownership of their own learning. They must develop personal goals for the practicum and understand how to communicate them clearly. To take this initiative student teachers must feel relaxed and secure with their cooperating teachers (keeping in mind the socio-political tensions as addressed in Chapter 5). Qualitative aspects of the interactions between teacher educator and novice can be more important than the quantity of discussion. Consider whether or not the listeners and speakers actually communicate and understand what the other is saying. For example, Figure 7.1 illustrates the complexities possible in interactions. It shows a situation in which a cooperating teacher has offered her student teacher more teaching time because it is her *intent* to communicate that her student teacher is ready for the challenge.

FIGURE 7.1:   Saying and Hearing Different Words (Intent and Effect)

However, the *effect* is lost because she does not clearly state why she is giving her more responsibility. In this case, the student teacher agrees to the suggestion with a smile even though the teacher's action leaves her feeling overwhelmed. The *effect* is that the student teacher believes the cooperating teacher is simply unloading a class while she catches up on other tasks. Overcoming such obstacles and building an environment of trust in a short period of time is not easy, even when the intentions are well meaning.

The Johari Window

A number of years ago, Joe Luft and Harry Ingram developed a framework, which they named the *Johari Window* (see Figure 7.2)[1]; it is useful for understanding some of the complexities underlying sensitive and straightforward communication.

FIGURE 7.2:   The Johari Window

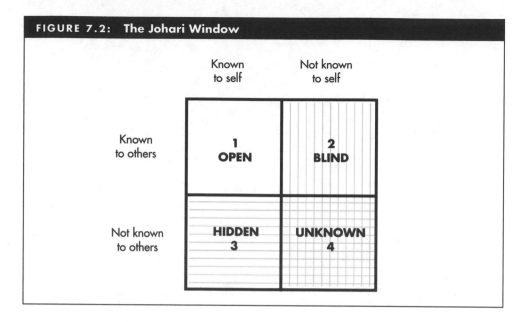

The Johari Window is designed to help you learn more about yourself and others, and to help others learn more about you in order to facilitate direct and substantive communication. The structure is a 2 x 2 matrix and represents what is known and not known to yourself and others. The *open* area contains knowledge that you and members of your practicum triad all recognise (e.g., gender, age, and ethnicity). The *blind* area represents knowledge available to others but not to yourself (e.g., characteristics or habits of which you are unaware). The *hidden* area holds knowledge to which you alone have access (e.g., personal feelings, private hopes, beliefs, and values). Finally, the *unknown* area contains knowledge unavailable to anyone in the group (e.g., denied feelings).

The open area of the Johari Window enables people to enjoy honest, open communication. When people who need to communicate are willing to expand their open area, Luft and Ingram propose that they will have a better chance of communicating effectively than if they kept the open area smaller. Revealing information helps the other person better understand your perspective. However, it would be foolish to suggest that people should reveal everything. We do not live in a perfect world, and each person must feel comfortable and safe prior to revealing insecurities. Because they have recognized expertise in teaching, and because they are ultimately responsible for evaluating the student teacher, teacher educators, whether cooperating teachers or faculty advisors, are in the best political position to establish an environment in which a student teacher can feel safe.

Student teachers can increase the size of their open area and reduce the size of their blind and hidden areas by being open to feedback and by revealing their preconceptions about teaching and learning (see Figure 7.3). Likewise, cooperating teachers or faculty advisors can begin to decrease the size of their blind and hidden areas by listening to their student teachers' concerns about the teaching assignment, as well as by disclosing their expectations and understanding of teaching.

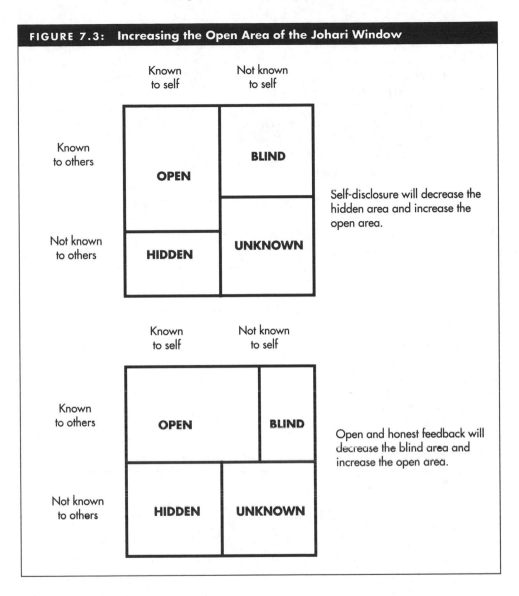

FIGURE 7.3: Increasing the Open Area of the Johari Window

Self-disclosure will decrease the hidden area and increase the open area.

Open and honest feedback will decrease the blind area and increase the open area.

THE NEED FOR STRUCTURE AND FLEXIBILITY

While it may seem incongruous at first glance, both structure and flexibility are essential in guiding a communicative practicum experience, which tends to make the process complicated for the participants. Structure is important because practicum experiences are often short, and conferences can regress into chat sessions, losing the necessary focus. Both novice teachers and teacher educators need to use time together productively by agreeing on what needs to be discussed. Lack of flexibility, however, can result in important issues being overlooked for the sake of expediency. As usual, balance is important.

In considering aspects of structure and flexibility in communication, it might be helpful to revisit the developmental perspectives of professional growth as outlined in Chapter 2: initial coping, taking on the professional role, and fostering pupil learning (see Figure 2.1). We will also consider the coping strategies raised in Chapter 5: overt compliance, critical compliance, accommodative resistance, resistant alteration, and transformative action. Teacher educators and student teachers might find these structures helpful in facilitating communication. As with any framework, however, flexibility rather than the blind adherence to structure is crucial. For example, in their initial phase of development, student teachers may be overwhelmed, even confused, and therefore fail to observe many of the salient points associated with teaching and learning. Communication is often about themselves rather than the pupils, and their hope is to survive this initial experience. A conferencing approach that provides explicit directions and goals is likely to assist them through the coping stage. It is an approach that parallels the teaching most student teachers experienced throughout their school years. Consequently, many student teachers find the approach reassuring rather than offensive, although cooperating teachers can find this technique difficult due to its non-collegial nature. The student teacher's concern for self is natural. As Kagan explains:

> The initial focus on self appears to be a necessary and crucial element in the first stage of teacher development. If this is true, then attempts by supervisors to shorten or abort a student teacher's period of inward focus may be counterproductive (Kagan, 1992, p. 155).

During the next stage of development, taking on the professional role, student teachers tend to be anxious about their performance and are more concerned with their teaching than the pupils' learning. They need feedback about themselves. Cooperating teachers can move towards a more collegial approach, letting the student teacher assume greater responsibility in decision-making by using the student teacher's recommendations to assist in navigating the appropriate sequence of events. The pair starts to work towards joint experimentation, negotiating and sharing their own perspectives, and addressing alternative ways to proceed.

In the third stage, fostering pupil learning, student teachers demonstrate a greater comfort level than before and are willing to experiment and attempt different teaching strategies to foster pupil learning. They shift their focus from self to pupil and from teaching to learning. They are ready to move on to deeper discussions examining why certain strategies appear to be more effective in some contexts and considering the benefits and limitations of various approaches. Student teachers should be encouraged to describe their own conclusions and recommendations, with the cooperating teacher requesting, and sometimes providing, clarification concerning future plans.

A cautionary note—one should not assume that student teachers' stages of development always correspond to early practicum experiences and then later experiences. Novice teachers (and, in fact, experienced teachers) tend to move among the stages depending on their comfort level and understanding in certain situations. For example, in the early practicum, a student teacher may begin to feel reassured and confident with a particular age of pupil, the subject matter, and the relationship with the cooperating teacher. Communication may be mutually beneficial and straightforward as novice and expert focus at a higher level of discussion, developing experimental teaching strategies in this environment. In the next practicum, the student teacher may be faced with a significantly dissimilar classroom, unknown subject matter, and a less open cooperating teacher personality. Student teachers then find themselves just trying to cope with or survive the new situation, as they seek to win the approval of the cooperating teacher. When the conferencing approach matches the student teacher's level of development and comfort—moving towards a joint experimental approach as the student teacher becomes more reflective, confident and informed—there is both structure and flexibility, and student teachers have opportunities to progress in a safe and supportive environment.

SOME FINAL THOUGHTS

Shulman (1986) has clearly demonstrated that knowing how to transform one's knowledge so that others can understand it is at the heart of teaching. Understanding a student's prior knowledge is paramount in this process. Consequently, teacher educators in faculties and in schools must be aware of their student teachers' prior knowledge in order to assist their understanding of teaching. Effective communication with student teachers is essential to uncover their preconceptions and makes it possible for cooperating teachers and faculty advisors to use appropriate analogies, illustrations, and representations for placing discussions of teaching and learning in contexts meaningful for their student teachers. Until honest, open lines of communication are established, it is doubtful that discussions resulting in professional growth and development will be meaningful or insightful.

Compromise, Conformity, or a Lack of Communication?

Patricia wondered if she was the only student teacher who thought there was something critically wrong with her first practicum experience. She wondered whether her anxieties were normal for student teachers who returned to school after a long absence, or if teaching might not be the career she expected it to be. Patricia was in her thirties and had decided to enter a faculty of education after eight years as a school psychometrist. Patricia had first considered this change three years earlier. As a psychometrist, she often visited classrooms. There she saw the joy on children's faces when they understood a new concept, and this convinced her that teaching would be more rewarding than testing.

Over the past three years she had discussed her plans with two close friends, one of whom was a teacher. She knew that initially she would have some financial difficulty, but had enough money saved to complete the one-year programme. Patricia was confident, believed she had a lot to offer children, and was enthusiastic about trying some of the many ideas she had seen in classrooms. She was also keen to attempt some of the new teaching strategies discussed during her first five weeks at the faculty. However, Patricia became disheartened towards the end of the first week when she realized that Shereen, her grade 1 cooperating teacher, expected her to follow the established classroom routines exactly. In fact, Patricia found that she disagreed with some of

Shereen's approaches, although she was not sure why, and wondered how she would make it through the final two weeks.

Shereen had taught successfully for 15 years in three elementary schools, and for the past six years had taught grade 1 at Elmwood School. Her colleagues and principal recognized Shereen as a very effective teacher who was highly organized and very caring of the children. In fact, several teachers in the school had already told Patricia what a wonderful teacher Shereen was and that she was lucky to work with her. Shereen had very strong views about the type of programme she believed her pupils needed, and wanted her views carried through "to the letter." As a student teacher herself, Shereen had followed the advice of her cooperating teachers and expected her student teachers to do the same. Shereen felt it was *her* classroom and that the children would become confused if changes occurred. Her routines were effective, and if student teachers could do as well as she did during their early years then they would be off to a sound start, and at least feel confident with one model of teaching. They could then attempt alternative strategies from a solid foundation.

During her second week Patricia occasionally tried out new techniques without first discussing them with Shereen. Whenever Patricia didn't follow Shereen's established routines the children often became confused and unsure of what to do. Shereen acknowledged to herself that Patricia generally handled the adverse situations well. However, she also knew that the difficulties would never have arisen if Patricia had just followed the established routines. In her feedback, Shereen told Patricia that what she was doing was inappropriate for these children at this point, and Patricia should follow the guidelines as they had discussed. However, Patricia wanted the freedom to follow her own creative ideas and then analyze her successes as well as her failures with Shereen. She had hoped her cooperating teacher would be open to discussing modifications that would help her understand her strengths as well as areas for improvement. Patricia appreciated the value of many of Shereen's strategies but did not want to follow her methods exactly, believing that conformity was not helping her develop to her full potential. Patricia was unsure, however, of how to express these feelings to Shereen. Patricia therefore complied as much as she could for the remainder of the practicum session, hoping for a different experience the next time. Shereen, on the other hand, felt that perhaps she had "gotten through" to Patricia after all.

By the end of the practicum session, Patricia and Shereen had a polite but restrained relationship. Patricia's report was above average and she was surprised to note that Shereen had recognized her potential as a creative teacher. Both felt somewhat uncomfortable and frustrated. Shereen believed that although it had been a struggle to convince Patricia to use appropriate strategies and routines, she had carried out her role to the best of her ability and provided Patricia with a solid foundation. Patricia left feeling she had missed something extremely important, and wondered if she had made the right choice about a career in teaching.

QUESTIONS

Framing, Reframing, and Exploring Solutions

1. Refer to the Johari Window and consider the relationship between Patricia and Shereen:
   a) What information is known to both Patricia and Shereen?
   b) What information is known to Shereen but not Patricia?
   c) What information is known to Patricia but not Shereen?
   d) What information is not known to either Patricia or Shereen that could be critical in the practicum?

2. Use the information from question one to complete (as much as is possible) the different areas of the Johari Window. Study the facts. If one or more of these facts had been in a different section of the window, how might the scenario described in the case study have been changed?

3. Ben-Peretz & Rumney (1991) found cooperating teachers viewed their student teachers "not as novice professionals, but as 'students' whose primary duty is to listen and learn" (p. 525). Use this quote to frame the situation from Shereen's perspective. What might Shereen have done to help Patricia better understand her approach?

4. Referring to the three stages of development as outlined in Chapter 2, through which many student teachers pass, at which of these three stages would you place Patricia? Provide at least two reasons for your decision, and then frame the situation from Patricia's perspective. What could Patricia have done to assist Shereen in recognizing the guidance she was looking for? How much *power* does Patricia have in this situation?

5. Reframe the situation from the perspective of the faculty advisor in the school. As the faculty advisor, what would be your response to Patricia's concerns? What strategies would help empower Patricia? What would be your reaction towards Shereen? Would your response differ if this were the second or third practicum, rather than the first session?

Personal Reflections and Connections

1. Place yourself in Patricia's shoes. Brainstorm all of the courses of action to assist you in having a successful practicum. Choose the best alternative, giving reasons for your choice.

2. Do you know of a situation similar to Patricia's and Shereen's? Discuss what happened, and what might have happened to improve the situation if the pair had been able to communicate with each other. What communication strategies might have been useful?

Reflections on Learning-to-Teach

1. Is this case a problem to be solved or a dilemma to be managed? How might the Johari Window be used to assist Patricia and Shereen in managing this dilemma, or resolving the problem?

2. What were the positive aspects of Patricia's placement and what were the shortcomings?

3. Was Patricia placed in an unreasonable position for this first placement? Explain your answer. What if this were the final practicum assignment?

4. As a cooperating teacher, how will you ensure that open communication occurs between you and your student teacher?

5. One strategy for opening lines of communication is an exchange of information at the first meeting. Student teachers can share their backgrounds and previous experiences, as well as what they are hoping to achieve in the practicum. Cooperating teachers can provide their student teachers with an overview of their philosophy of teaching and learning, a brief description of the pupils (especially those with special needs), or some classroom routines, together with a rationale. Discuss what you think is appropriate to share at an introductory meeting.

6. Discuss the various pitfalls in the communication process and ways for you to overcome each of them.

7. Discuss why you are for or against having student teachers wear a *bug-in-the-ear*. Reflect on the positive and negative aspects of this technological device.

ENDNOTES

1. Figure 7.2 from *Group Processes: An Introduction to Group Dynamics, Third Edition* by Joseph Luft. Copyright © 1984 by Joseph Luft. Reprinted by permission of Mayfield Publishing Company.

ISSUES OF GENDER, RACE, AND CLASS IN LEARNING-TO-TEACH

Novice teachers and teacher educators must become cognizant of and proactive about the diffuse issues surrounding gender, race, and class, in order to further awareness, action in social justice, and equity in the educational system. Our increasingly diverse society has complicated, yet greatly enhanced the process of learning-to-teach, and teacher educators and novice teachers must actively consider what we must do and teach and how we must act in order to facilitate social justice in our classrooms.

We purposely grouped gender, race, and class in this chapter; we have developed the topics simultaneously to help denote and emphasize their interrelationship. In fact, as they learn more about and value our diverse North American culture, most informed researchers now base their writing on the intersection of gender, race, and class because issues and implications for one cannot be discussed realistically without awareness of the others. It is not by chance in North American society that those from cultures other than the dominant group find themselves living in poverty and that most of those are women. For example, most current feminist writers realize that the issues that affect the women about whom they write are also imprinted and complicated by cultural background and socioeconomic status. Frequently, discussions of any one of these three in isolation (i.e., gender, race, or class) exclude or minimize the connections required to come to a comprehensive awareness of the impact of these social issues on teaching and learning. Ongoing and informed reading, experience, discussion, and reflection are necessary for educators to become competent teachers of *all* pupils, and novice teachers, whether in school or university classrooms. In fact, this may prove to be one area in which experienced teacher educators find themselves learning-to-teach alongside their novice colleagues.

The topic of this chapter, Gender, Race, and Class in Learning-to-Teach, is complex and multifaceted, even contentious. (In fact, it is important to point out that the deliberation of gender, race and class—like most of the other issues we have tackled in this book—is far more complex than can be dealt with in this one chapter.) The following discussion is meant to establish a framework to further awareness, to promote action, and to provide a set of lenses with which to view the case studies that follow. In this chapter we begin by asking our readers and ourselves to reflect on and reconsider who we are in order to come to this topic with as open and informed an understanding as possible. We seek to come to an awareness of what we believe, and how we act based on our own cultured, gendered, and socioeconomic background. Then we discuss some of the issues about class, gender, and race in the context of learning-to-teach, considering how gender, race, and class influence each person in the community of learners. We conclude by examining how the community of professional practice might take action to enrich practices in schools.

EXAMINING WHO WE ARE

We are who we are! And it is critically important that we examine just what that means personally in order for us to understand who we are as teachers and how we interact. We may be naive enough to actually believe we have succeeded in coming to this point in our lives because we have worked hard and broken through barriers to achieve our goals. But the height of the barriers and the breadth of the obstacles we have faced and overcome have been influenced by broader agendas of race, class, and gender within our society. For some the barriers and obstacles have been inconvenient, for others almost impossible, and for those who would be here but are not, insurmountable. We are who we are and it is imperative that we consider our values, beliefs, and ideologies if we are to become effective teachers of all pupils in the twenty-first century.

Our own ethnicity, gender, and socioeconomic status define who we are and how we see ourselves as well as how others see us. It is impossible for any of us to consider issues about learning as they relate to others in an unbiased or uninformed way. No matter how aware of sociopolitical issues we are, we have been shaped by where we have come from, the circumstances of our birth, our childhood, our gender, our neighbourhoods, our own schooling, and by the way we unconsciously or, otherwise, consider others in relation to ourselves. Our frames for viewing situations are ingrained within each of us and even though we may try to reframe a situation we should realize that because our values, beliefs, and ideologies are entrenched they limit our possibilities.

Issues of social justice and equity in education are complicated by the fact that the majority of teachers and student teachers in North America continue to be a homogeneous group of white, female, middle-class adults (McIntyre & Byrd, 1996). For the most part, we are products of and have succeeded in accepting, confirming, and propagating the values and ideologies of the dominant, white, Eurocentric society. Therefore, as we consider the issues in this chapter, it is important to remember *who we really are,* and to wrestle with that character. The following exercise will help us (Figure 8.1). Since the questions require all of us to look back on our lives, it is crucial that we are as thorough and thoughtful as possible in considering our responses to these questions. Write down your responses in point form.

FIGURE 8.1:   Discovering Who We Really Are

1. Who are you (i.e., ethnicity, gender, and social class)?

2. What was your childhood like?
   What privileges did you experience as a child? What disadvantages? Why?

3. What advantages and disadvantages do you experience now? Why?

4. How has your background affected your pre- and post-secondary education?
   Your career choices?

5. How do you view learners who are different from you in cultural, social, and/or gendered ways?

Use the information you have gathered as you read on; it will assist you to frame your own situation from a personal and informed viewpoint while helping you interpret the concepts presented in this chapter.

GENDER, RACE, AND CLASS: EXAMINING THE ISSUES

Our educational system, like our communities, exists in an increasingly diverse environment. This includes pupils, parents, and (too few) teachers with different cultural roots, socioeconomic background, political ideals, views of gender, sexualities, ideological values, beliefs about valued knowledge, and so on. In fact, such diversity has long existed but educators have only recently begun to give it the attention required to begin to educate all pupils fairly and adequately and to recognize the value that minority beliefs provide. We all live in a state of tension as we value, yet critique, our single, dominant culture while perceiving a new richness in our society. Whereas at one point educators believed that our dominant society's values were the only ones to be inculcated into its learners, we are slowly coming to realize the resonance and value of alternative cultures' ideologies and to recognize the positive impact they have. Even with this new awareness, the process of transforming the system to accommodate, respect, and value difference will be arduous.

Pierre Bourdieu (1977) who introduced the concept of *habitus* can help us understand how diversity is treated in society. Habitus encompasses the way in which culture becomes embedded in an individual, becoming a disposition to act one way or another. It includes the *cultural, academic,* and *linguistic capital,* which are at the core of a person's behaviour; the habitus is shaped by the ideologies and norms of the person's culture, gender, and social class.

Cultural capital involves ideologies and beliefs, including religious, political, familial, and so on that are inculcated into the individual through the home, community and, sometimes, schools. In North America, *traditional* values have been centred around the Judaeo-Christian principles of the dominant Eurocentric white society. Those who have been brought up to believe in and live by different principles are disadvantaged in many ways. Complicating this problem is the fact that members of minority groups may not even be cognizant of the values of the dominant class and thus, may not even be aware that their own values, which are frequently unconscious or tacit, conflict with beliefs of the *other*.

Academic capital refers to the value that a community places on education. For example, the dominant class in North American society values a public or private formalized education for all of its citizens and places even higher worth on a university education. Other communities resident in North America place higher priority on the education that occurs within the community and may even devalue public education because it seems to work against the values of their culture, confusing their children. While members of the dominant class endeavour to *save* the children of alternative communities by forcing them to conform to the dominant educational framework, members of alternative communities frequently rebel against those norms that undermine the basic tenets of their community.

Linguistic capital refers specifically to the use of the first or dominant language within our society. A person's operative use of language specifically denotes his/her level of education as well as his/her place in our stratified society. Members of the informed or privileged dominant class enter schooling tacitly aware that there are formal and informal uses of language, and know implicitly or learn very quickly when to use the appropriate conventions in language, both verbal and written. Those who enter school with another first language or with a limited background in the use of language are disadvantaged and may not even be aware of it.

Such cultural, linguistic, or academic capital is of great advantage in schooling for children from the dominant culture. Children from alternative cultures bring capital which is frequently ignored or devalued (not always intentionally) and so they must begin to assimilate and learn the *capital* of the dominant society as well as the curriculum of their lessons. Given this viewpoint, education is seen as more supportive of those who have the valued capital and disparaging of those who do not. Because many of these cultural attributes are tacit, it is difficult for socially and culturally different pupils or teachers to develop the indispensable capital during the school years when the curriculum and mode of instruction begins with the assumption that everyone has the *socially acceptable* background. Social institutions such as schools value the habitus of the middle or upper class and they implicitly develop curriculum and expectations as if everyone had access to the same habitus, ignoring or being unaware of the invisible but weighty barriers that curtail growth and advancement for people from alternative backgrounds. Education is seen through this perspective as mainly a process of socialization.

> The possession of the dominant habitus then, in Bourdieu's terminology, becomes a form of *symbolic capital* and its legitimation as a natural rather than a social gift becomes an exercise in *symbolic violence* by the school in its power to dominate disadvantaged groups. (May, 1994, p. 24).

Complicating Bourdieu's thesis is the development of habitus as pupils grow into adolescence and adulthood. Individuals within subordinate groups may find themselves at odds with the capital of their own culture, subject to symbolic violence within their own culture, as they learn about and are forced to acquiesce to the traditional ideologies of the dominant group in order to *succeed* by current society's standards. This forced assimilation creates hard choices for diverse learners and teachers to make as they determine their outcomes in a society that may not be as tolerant as we would hope. At the same time, this shaping of a new identity estranges them from their own birth culture. Simultaneously, individuals within the dominant group who challenge the norms of cultural and academic capital of their own advantaged group may find themselves excluded and isolated. For example, student teachers of the dominant culture with alternative beliefs and lifestyles (e.g., in terms of sexual preferences) may be marginalized and forced to worry about evaluation of their practice as teachers if their life values are made public. Thus, schools may be seen to educate in order to socialize. Such socialization creates stratification within our schools that spreads into society.

Stratification in schools occurs as a result of the way in which schools function. Schools select and certify the workforce, and through streaming of classes prepare some students (usually from the disadvantaged classes and minority cultures) to assume working-class attitudes and to labour through a skills-oriented, non-academic curriculum. Meanwhile, schools prepare others (usually from the dominant mid-upper-class population) in upper-class thinking for intellectual, highly-paid positions, thus maintaining the stratification of society (Apple, 1982). Schools maintain privilege by passing on the norms of the dominant culture and defining them as the legitimate knowledge; schools legitimate new knowledge, new classes, and social strata in the context of the dominant society. The dominant values of society are the dominant values of the schools and are defended by our democratically selected governments.

Consider again the activity that you completed at the beginning of this chapter. Now think about the concept of *habitus* as it relates to you (Figure 8.2). After you gather the information, continue to think about it as you read and reflect on the issues raised further in this chapter. What impact might this information have on you as a teacher?

The concept of habitus, educational socialization, and stratification leads one to theorize that there are two power structures in society—the privileged and the oppressed. The privileged dominate the oppressed—not always intentionally, by the way—and, therefore, do not allow minority interests to be integrated into the mainstream. To be successful, members of the marginal cultures (and, by members of marginal cultures, we mean cultural and social minorities as well as members of other disadvantaged groups such as women, disabled people, persons with alternative sexual orientations, and so on) have to learn and internalize

---

FIGURE 8.2: Discover Your Capital

1. Describe the cultural capital of your home. How did it blend with your activities as a primary (or older) pupil in school? Did you at any point feel any tensions between the cultural expectations of your home and your school?

2. Describe the academic capital of your background. What expectations for academic success were placed on you by parents/guardians/others? How congruent were these expectations with those of your teachers? Of yourself? How many people in your direct family have a university education? What percentage of your friends has or will have a university education?

3. Describe the linguistic capital of your home. How does the everyday conversational language of your home environment compare with that used in your school classrooms? How does the language of your friends compare to that of your parents? The teachers you had in elementary or secondary school?

4. Think honestly. What impact has your habitus had on your attitudes toward others (e.g., classmates who dropped out of school, who did not go on to university, street people, members of other cultures)?

the ideologies and customs of the privileged or the powerful in society. May (1994) acknowledges that such an ideology is functional because the power of the capitalist class determines both the explicit and hidden curriculum in schools. As such, researchers and educators are urged to question current practice and to find collective, collaborative, and formal ways to help or *emancipate* those who are oppressed in overt and implicit practices both in classroom teaching and in the education of new teachers. The term *emancipate* means more than simply liberating some person or group; it implies that all persons, given opportunity and appropriate support, can liberate themselves from that which oppresses them, be it poverty, ethnicity, and/or gender. And, as a result of this perspective and because we live in a country formally committed to recognizing and enshrining minority rights, reality in the educational system is being reclaimed in a different and controversial way, although it may take a long time for us to see the results.

Teacher education is subject to the same constraining structural norms, ideologies, and values that govern schools. Just as schools are premised on the fundamental beliefs of the dominant society, so too are teacher education institutions. Popkewitz (1987) notes that the same rituals of public schooling are institutionalized in teacher education facilities: "Conduct is structured by codes of culture which govern the ways in which people think, feel, and 'see' and act toward the practices of schooling" (p. 2).

Corson (1993) notes that just as schooling evolved to socialize youngsters into society, so too did a specific group emerge who had the authority and power to develop and implement the curriculum (overt and hidden) and the norms of the schooling that would inculcate and reinforce society's ideologies and beliefs into the minds of students. New teachers were trained to take over these responsibilities, overtly through such activities as teaching lessons during *practice* teaching and subtly by maintaining the norms of the culture through classroom management (Popkewitz, 1987). If field experiences in schools are for student teachers to practice and be evaluated on their ability to convey the codes of the system to students, then student teachers who understand the structures and codes of the dominant society in education may be better able to demonstrate these attributes and be more successful at teaching. Student teachers who come from a different or minority background, be it gender, race, or class, may be impeded in understanding what is important and may not be able to achieve the desired results unless they become assimilated into the norms of the dominant culture.

As mentioned previously, one complicating factor in considering gender, race, and class in learning-to-teach is the composition of teacher education classes. Student teachers, cooperating teachers, and the university-based teacher educators continue to be largely a homogeneous grouping of white, middle class people across North America (McIntyre & Byrd, 1996). Thus, if new teachers are rewarded for conforming, then change is unlikely until they can view the system in a critical manner. Student teachers who attempt to question the norms and structures generally do so at personal risk. Townsend and Robinson (1994) confirm the homogeneity of the teaching population but point out the problems that politicians have when confronted with such a problem. While politicians note the lack of diversity in the teaching force and recognize that minorities may have been and continue to be disadvantaged, they have done little about the situation.

> The notion of risk to contextual stability here enters into policy makers' talk. Interviewees tell me that, until recently, the department has been concerned that greater aggressiveness in affirmative action might have been divisive and therefore potentially destabilizing (p. 155).

In short, there appears to be recognition of the need for more effective affirmative action programs to diversify the teaching population, but paradoxically, the implementation of affirmative action programs remains unlikely because they might upset the status quo of the dominant culture.

WORKING TOGETHER TOWARD RESOLUTION

There is evidence, however, that change is afoot as evidenced in some preservice university programs. Topics of social action and justice are becoming fundamental components of mandatory courses; courses in alternative pedagogies are becoming more prevalent. Instructors and student teachers are influenced by writers who encourage us to consider viewing our world in alternative ways. Paolo Freire is one researcher/writer who provides some insight for those of us learning-to-teach through his work with poor, adult learners in South America. Freire (1985) describes government educational programs designed to teach adult illiterate peasant farmers to read and write. Although the exercise appeared to be commendable and a just attempt to liberate these adults from their prison of ignorance, Freire exposes the pitfalls of such an intervention. He shows that the teaching methods used were irrelevant in helping the adults learn anything more than just the mechanics of reading and writing. The adults learned nothing about their situation or their place in society.

To help the peasant students learn to read, the teachers used a curriculum that included statements, such as "The birds fly," which were of little illuminative use to them in genuine *learning*. In his situation, Freire (1985) argued for a meaningful curriculum for his peasants that would make use of what he calls *generative words,* in order to open dialogue with the peasants about their role in society. This curriculum would form a critical component in their learning so that they could use the new knowledge not only to read and write, but also to discuss ways of freeing themselves from poverty. Freire calls for an emancipatory curriculum for pupils and teachers. He reminds us that the peasants develop their own way of seeing and understanding the world, according to cultural patterns marked by the ideology of dominant groups in their society. As a result their ways of thinking are adapted by the very behaviour that conditions their thinking, having been developed and crystallized over a long period of time (Freire, 1985). Thus, even with this emancipatory curriculum, the education process is complex and may not be as successful as we would like.

What does this mean to us in learning-to-teach? Certainly, we are not claiming that our student teachers are peasants; they are not illiterate and they can have and use voice if they wish to do so in a supportive environment. But, they have been trained to see the world in certain ways (Lortie, 1975) and have been successful as pupils themselves in accommodating that view of society. Student teachers have been conditioned to the norms of the system after thousands of hours of experience in classrooms before they enter teaching. Yet, for the most part, their experience as pupils is not typical of the pupils they will teach. In fact, many may have chosen teaching as a career because of a holistic acceptance of the educational system, the inner need to pass on the knowledge to others, or the urge to exercise power over others. Thus, before they even begin teaching, it appears that new teachers may willingly contribute to maintaining the status quo. We need to work consciously to open our minds to difference and diversity, to be aware of the position of privilege that we have, and to give voice to novice teachers in order to give their pupils a fair chance.

Working with student teachers in such emancipatory ways may not be easy, not only for the reasons listed above. We have heard our own student teachers complain about their teacher education classes in the university setting, about how meaningless they often are because we talk about framing and reframing issues in education and managing dilemmas rather than providing solutions that work. Some novice teachers see their role as one in which, as teachers, they need to maintain power and control in schools. Some seek a curriculum that guarantees success in the classroom, a methodological *bags of tricks* to help them at least maintain the status quo. Success in student teaching is an excellent report from the supervising teacher, and an excellent report is truly powerful because it is the most influential route to employment in the system. Supervising teachers, on the other hand, hold all of the power in that it is they who determine who will receive the excellent teaching reports that will permit beginning teachers to obtain teaching positions (see Chapter 6); they are, in fact, the gatekeepers of the profession (see Chapter 11). To assist student teachers to find success in alternative and risky teaching methodologies, teacher educators need to put their own theories into practice. We must all strive to recreate the situation in which the participants live and must rethink our own thinking in terms of those disempowered by the system. While we are not about to recommend that we throw everything away that we have in our system, we encourage a thorough critique and a need to show our student teachers how to do the same.

Power or authority in teaching is frequently measured in terms of a classroom of quiet and compliant pupils who can regurgitate the content that teachers put into their minds. Freire (1985) refers to this type of teaching as a *banking* method that visualizes pupils as empty vessels waiting to be filled. If pupils are perceived as empty vessels, then student teachers also must be vessels waiting to be given the codified knowledge of teaching, which they then impart to their pupils. In his advocacy of generative words, Freire champions the people's words and demands that they become an integral part of the teaching. Succinctly, Freire says, we all have a lot to learn from peasants, and if we refuse to do so, we can't teach them anything (p. 25).

Thus, he exhorts teacher educators to challenge the community (student teachers and teacher educator colleagues) to decode the structures, language, and discourse (of the educational establishment). In Freire's terms then, by understanding the codification's deep structure, student teachers as well as experienced teachers can understand the dialectic that exists between the categories presented in the surface structure. They may also see the unity between the "surface and deep structures" (p. 52) in order to reconstruct their former practice and become capable of an emancipated way of engaging in teaching and learning. Freire (1985) emphasizes that the relationship between the theoretical context and the concrete context has to be made real. The researcher/educator's role is to propose problems about the codified existential situation to help the learners arrive at a more critical view of educational reality in order to resist current practice. Aspiring teachers must be confronted at the outset with examination and re-examination of who they are as teachers because learning to teach is personally constructed (Britzman, 1991). Student teachers' voices must be acknowledged, heard, encouraged, and even challenged in the discourse according to Sumara and Luce-Kapler (1996) because learning-to-teach means engaging in acts of forgetting, discarding, silencing, and ignoring (p. 78).

If the curriculum of learning-to-teach does not include such emancipatory practices, then student teachers remain as prisoners throughout their own preservice education.

While universities may be seen as liberalizing institutions, when it comes to using methods such as inquiry and critical reflection for student learning, they really are very conservative. University courses are generally offered and evaluated in a depository way, to further Freire's notions of the banking method, which directs certain limited types of learning. Simultaneously, in the practicum, teacher education students are socialized into the conservative norms of the schools (Feiman-Nemser & Buchmann, 1987). In developing a solution to these problems, Cochran-Smith (1991) advocates an idealistic model of *collaborative resonance* in teacher education where student teachers learn in mutually constructed learning communities, developed between the university and the schools, where the purpose is not how to teach but how to continue learning. She notes that the way to link theory and practice is through a self-critical program where systematic inquiry about learning (both teacher and student) is paramount. This suggestion resonates with our concept of the scholarship of pedagogy as outlined in Chapter 1. Such comments as noted above might be perceived as revolutionary for student teachers and teacher educators but we see them as relevant. If teacher education is to become more than teacher socialization intended to educate pupils according to dominant norms and ideologies, then beginning teachers must be made aware of the tensions and be given opportunity to engage in the scholarship of pedagogy so they may be released from the forces that socialize. They need safe access to Freire's generative language of educational discourse. Indeed, this release may help them begin the process of decoding the dialogue of power, so that they can arrive at a critical view of the reality in education in order to provide an optimal learning environment.

Making the Grade: But What If the Grade Is Just Too Steep?

Gihajnne was the first of her family ever to finish secondary school and to go to university. Her parents, both non-English speaking immigrants who worked 10–14 hours a day at hard physical labour to support their extended family, were so proud of her accomplishments. The youngest of seven children, she was quite aware that she carried a huge responsibility. All of her siblings worked in minimum wage jobs, some were married with their own young, growing families, and most were happy. But all just managed to scrape by. Her parents and family were so proud that one of their own would someday be a respected professional. Giha felt that her family and the community perceived her as the one who would save her family merely because she was enrolled in a local university program. It seemed that almost each week, her mother and father would ask her what she planned to do when she graduated. Giha observed that even her own cultural community, most of whom were just managing to survive themselves, beamed at her when she came to events and always wished her well, bestowing blessings on her quite publicly. At times, members of her community would even ask her advice about important personal decisions and she felt most uncomfortable giving her opinion.

Giha enjoyed her schooling and realized that the only way that she could go to university was to win some scholarship money and to carry a full-time job outside of school. She was determined to get a degree, to find a well-paying professional career, and to do her part to help out her struggling family. As she proceeded through first, second, and then third year, Giha realized that she had little idea of what career to pursue. She was taking a social science degree with a major in sociology. As she entered her fourth and final year, she felt exhausted. Over the summer, she had carried two jobs, working seven days a week and as many as fourteen hours a day. When she finally got home, she would often meet her equally exhausted parents just coming in. She tried to help out her mother by cleaning, cooking, and caring for her little nieces/nephew whose parents were on the night shift. Since English was rarely spoken in their home, she tried to read to the little ones in English as often as she could because she believed it might help them do better in school.

Two weeks into her fourth year, Giha was determined to make a decision about her future before the end of that month. After attending some of the professional school recruitment sessions and talking briefly to a very busy academic counsellor, Giha decided to focus on teaching. Initially she thought she might want to become a secondary teacher but when she discovered that she did not have the appropriate teaching subjects, she opted to apply for a generalist elementary teaching program. As she completed the lengthy application process, wrote out the cheque for the stiff application fees, and sent it off in the mail, Giha felt a sense of relief. Now she could tell her parents that she was going to be a teacher. She knew they would be so proud of her.

At the faculty of education, Giha found herself in a very different academic community. She was taking courses in curriculum areas she had not even thought about since high school, and she realized that not only would she have to learn that content but also how to teach it! She had not really thought about what the program would involve. Suddenly she found she was forced to think about herself as the teacher of a primary classroom, working with 25 or 30 young children who would believe she knew what she was doing. As her first student teaching block approached in a grade 2 classroom, she felt a real sense of apprehension. She felt she had no one to really talk to. Her parents would have no idea what she was talking about. She had no real friends at school or in her community to talk to. She suddenly realized that she was a loner; she had never had time for a social life. She did not want to talk to any of her professors for fear she would be seen as a weak candidate and so she never volunteered to speak in their classes. She felt truly alone in a very confusing world of teacher education. But that feeling soon evaporated each day as she ran out of her university class to arrive on time for her work as a server at a local diner.

During student teaching, Giha observed her cooperating teacher very carefully and planned her teaching assignments meticulously in the early hours of the morning after working another eight-hour shift. The teaching went well and her cooperating teacher seemed pleased. She always had many positive comments to make as well as some very realistic suggestions for improvement. However, Giha felt her cooperating teacher was being too nice and she could see how much she needed to improve. On the other hand, she did not feel at ease talking about teaching with such an experienced professional. At the end of the placement, Giha accepted a fair report and looked forward to getting back to her university classes.

Back in class, she heard her colleagues talking excitedly about their experiences. In fact, the halls, the cafeteria, and her classes buzzed with enthusiastic chatter. She did not find her way into any of the conversations and she realized that she was anything but enthusiastic about her experience. As the term progressed, Giha began to feel somewhat depressed about herself and her career choice. She began to realize she could not become excited about teaching for the next 35 years of her life. Should she quit? But what would she tell her family? She just could not bear to see the disappointment in their eyes or in the eyes of her community. Should she just continue on and try to finish the program? What if she failed? That would certainly be worse.

In mid-November, Giha asked for an appointment with the faculty's academic counsellor. She explained her problem as carefully as she could and asked about withdrawing. She learned that if she made the decision to withdraw at this point, she could do so without academic penalty and would receive a modest refund of her fees. If she waited any later, she would certainly lose all of her tuition and have a permanent grade of failure on her transcript. The academic counsellor outlined all of the options and asked her to consider her decision most carefully. As another week dragged by, Giha began to feel physically ill and could not even bear to go to classes. She felt she had no choice but to withdraw from the program, which she did. Giha went out immediately to look for another minimum-wage job to fill in her now empty days. As she left the faculty of education for the last time, she felt relief on one hand, but a sense of foreboding about what she was doing to her family on the other. She considered alternatives for a while—running away from home, suicide, lying to them. She felt totally alone and empty inside.

QUESTIONS

Framing, Reframing, and Exploring Solutions

1. Review the case study again to outline the problems that Giha faces.
2. How does her gender, race, and class make her particularly vulnerable in this case study?
3. Review Bourdieu's concept of habitus. How does his framework of cultural capital, academic capital, and linguistic capital help us to understand Giha's situation?
4. Review Freire's framework of education in light of the illiterate peasants with whom he worked? How can this conceptual framework be applicable to teacher education for a situation like Giha's?
5. What realistic and satisfactory solutions could Giha seek in her future?

6. Are there supports that the university system, the school system, and the community could/should have had to assist Giha in managing her dilemmas? What are they?

Personal Reflections and Connections

1. Have you ever been forced into a difficult situation because of expectations placed on you? Whose expectations were they and what did they relate to? Describe the situation and tell how you reacted. Now that the situation is behind you and you have time to think about it, how might you have reacted?

2. Have you ever had an advantage because of your gender, race, or class? Describe the situation.

3. Articulate your own values of schooling, thinking about both teachers and learners. How are your values explicitly and implicitly demonstrated in your curriculum and in your teaching methods?

4. How might your values be different or similar to the values of your pupils, your colleagues, your cooperating teacher, the school administration, or the government?

5. Consider carefully your expectations of your pupils based on their gender. What expectations do you have of the male students in your class(es)? Of the female students? How do they differ?

6. Consider your expectations in relation to the socioeconomic status and cultural background of your students. How does this affect your teaching and your evaluation of student progress?

7. Canvass your own school or university community to find the supports that exist for students with concerns or vulnerabilities. How well is the system working? How do you know for sure?

Broader Reflections on Learning-to-Teach

1. We live in a society where support mechanisms are supposed to be in place to help people who are victimized by circumstances. If this is true, why do we hear time and again that vulnerable people do not find success in using these supports?

2. How can we, not only as teachers but as members of a society that seeks to address issues of social justice, identify and assist those who require support.

3. Do teachers really want to hear voices in our society that are different from their own? Give an example of a situation where you have observed a teacher develop practices that support marginalized pupils. Why did this strategy work? What were its limitations?

4. What is essential knowledge for schools? How can a provincial curriculum or base of knowledge be developed for schools that meets high standards yet is still inclusive?

Shahid's Primary Dilemma: Touch in the Classroom

One day on recess yard duty, during Shahid's first primary teaching assignment as a student teacher, a little girl named Maggie came running up to him. She had fallen and skinned her little knees, and was crying. Maggie was obviously hurt and frightened. She instinctively reached out to Shahid to be held and comforted but he responded by stepping back. Instead he gave Maggie a stiff pat on the back when she hugged his knees, and then gently pushed her away. While Maggie backed away, looking hurt and disappointed, Shahid realized that his response left him feeling inadequate as a teacher to this young child. He thought that if he gave her a hug, he would get in trouble, especially since he was in view of other staff members and parent volunteers on recess duty. Although he had always wanted to be a primary teacher, he had heard that males who wanted to teach young children were seen as suspect or questionable.

Shahid had always been naturally affectionate with children, and as a student teacher, he noticed how the pupils in his grade 1 class craved touch. He just had to sit on the floor, and within a matter of seconds, there would be a couple of children on his lap. Shahid was warned by peers and teachers he knew that men in primary grades had to be very careful about touching pupils. He was quite aware that there was a current climate of concern about male primary teachers as latent sexual predators. Shahid felt torn by his natural affection towards the children and concern for his own personal protection. He also felt angry that his cooperating teacher, a woman, could confidently touch children without any fear of reproach, while he had to be extremely careful and reflect on every incident. He felt that this affected his ability to be spontaneous with the students.

While Shahid had heard that some female teachers were not very positive towards males in primary teaching positions, Susan Lambert was a very encouraging, helpful cooperating teacher but she had little advice to give Shahid with this problem. She understood his concerns and suggested that he speak with the one other male teacher on staff. This sounded like a good idea, and that afternoon Shahid made an arrangement to speak with an experienced male teacher, Jason Field.

Jason was able to relate immediately to Shahid's difficulties. In his many years of teaching experience, he had developed strategies for dealing with touch in the classroom. Jason felt that the children in his classes did need to be touched, but in a way that was not dangerous for him. He made a point of shaking hands with the students before they left for the day. Pats on the back were also appropriate. When Shahid related the incident with Maggie in the schoolyard, Jason told him of an approach he had developed. He would kneel down to the child's eye level and warmly take her hands, while listening intently. Jason suggested that this was a way to keep the child from feeling rejected, and also allowed Jason to connect and comfort a child without being put in a compromising situation. Shahid was relieved to know that other male teachers felt similarly, and that there might be some alternative and creative ways to deal with touch in the classroom. He just wished he had thought of those strategies earlier in the day as he remembered the disconsolate look in Maggie's eyes.

QUESTIONS

Framing, Reframing, and Exploring Solutions

1. Review this case to study the issues that Shahid faces.
2. Was Shahid justified in feeling concern about touching the pupils in his class? Why? Why not?
3. What other solutions might Shahid find to address his concerns?
4. What are strategies that both male and female teachers can use to deal with such situations?

Personal Reflections and Connections

1. In what ways have the values and norms of our North American society perpetuated concerns about male teachers in the primary division? What intersection with race and class might male teachers face?
2. Identify other areas of sensitivity related to gender, socioeconomic status or ethnicity that teachers face in their work as professionals in the classroom.
3. How can cooperating teachers assist student teachers in understanding sensitive areas of teachers' work?
4. Have you had any experiences in your teaching like Shahid's? Use the Critical Teaching Incident framework (Figure 1.1) to outline your case and share it with a colleague.

Broader Reflections on Learning-to-Teach

1. Will having more male teachers in early years classrooms alleviate or aggravate the dilemma which Shahid faced? Support your answer using one of the conceptual frameworks of Freire or Bourdieu as described in the beginning section of this chapter. Find some primary and secondary sources about your researcher's work to augment your answer.

OPENING THE DOOR TO TODAY'S INCLUSIVE CLASSROOM

All learners have different requirements and expectations. As Murray (1993, p. 173) states, "Fewer and fewer students fit neatly into the traditional teacher-centred classrooms of the past." The dynamics of today's inclusive classrooms can confuse new teachers, who need well-informed teacher educators to guide them through the many complex uncertainties they will encounter. During courses at the faculty, it often becomes apparent that student teachers' conceptions of the special-needs classroom do not match today's reality. Many student teachers believe they will be assisting pupils who have minor learning difficulties, pupils like those they remember from their own school days. When they realize they might have to teach pupils who are blind, deaf, physically impaired, mentally disabled or behaviourally disordered, many feel overwhelmed. As one student teacher remarked, "I just cannot be expected to do all that!"

This chapter explores some of the important issues and characteristics of inclusive classrooms and offers opportunities for reflection and discussion. Throughout, we recommend that you use the concepts presented in Chapter 3 to frame and reframe the situations. Attempt to view concerns as might the members of the inclusive classroom. We also suggest you revisit Chapter 4 because many of the issues discussed in this chapter cannot be resolved; they have to be managed so that teaching and learning can continue.

Prior to opening the door of today's inclusive classroom, it is important for teacher educators and student teachers to consider two questions:

- What are the preconceptions and implicit theories of novice teachers regarding special-needs learners?

- How do novice teachers interpret the term *fair*?

When contemplating the first question, one might well think about a perspective from Clark (1988), who proposes that "[t]eachers' implicit theories tend to be eclectic aggregations of cause-effect propositions from many sources, rules of thumb, generalizations drawn from personal experience, beliefs, values, biases, and prejudices"(p. 6). Research on the education of new teachers indicates clearly that the preconceptions and implicit theories they hold when they enter faculties of education have a significant impact on their growth and development (Clark, 1988; Hollingsworth, 1989; Laine, 1991; Zeichner & Liston, 1987). Schoonmaker's (1998) study seems to confirm "the significance of surfacing, critiquing, and beginning the process of reconstructing prior images of teaching" (p. 584) if novice teachers are to make purposeful connections between theory and practice, and be able to explore pedagogy in a worthwhile fashion. Surfacing, critiquing, and reconstructing our beliefs and attitudes regarding the advantages and disadvantages of inclusion are essential components of teacher education.

Student teachers' attitudes and beliefs regarding inclusive education differ (see Crealock & Laine, 1996). In order to challenge these views, all teacher educators have the responsibility of raising issues and creating cognitive dissonance. At the same time everyone involved must remember that conflict resolution takes time and can seldom be accomplished satisfactorily in isolation or in a non-supportive environment. New teachers have to feel secure if they are to take risks and disclose their thoughts and beliefs. Yet until they do, professional growth and development will be hampered.

The second question, "How do novice teachers interpret the term *fair*?" is more complex than it might appear on the surface. Richard Lavoie (1990) suggests that, "Fair does not mean that every child gets the same treatment, but that every child gets what he or she needs." This description frequently creates unease for those who believe that being fair implies treating everyone in the same manner. It would be useful to reflect for a few minutes on Lavoie's statement, noting what you consider it means to be fair in today's inclusive classroom. It is a notion to which we will return.

As you read this chapter, revisit your responses to these two questions because there will not be one correct answer for most issues. Educational dilemmas are seldom black or white and the lens one uses to view a situation often determines the shade of grey. Openness, inquisitiveness, and empathy are vital qualities for teacher educators who want to assist new teachers by fostering thoughtful inquiry.

DIVERSE LEARNERS IN TODAY'S INCLUSIVE CLASSROOMS

Inclusive education is a philosophy suggesting that all pupils have worthwhile contributions to make, and everyone benefits from the associations which become possible in the inclusive classroom.

> The current trend toward greater inclusion of special-needs students in today's regular classroom has significantly complicated the nature of teaching. The greatest challenge for teachers is to create educational environments that provide structure as well as flexibility for students and that enhance the learning of all students (Andrews, 1996, p. 4).

Teaching pupils in an inclusive environment is not easy. As a result, teachers, especially novice teachers, need support from a variety of sources if they are to help as many pupils as possible to reach their full potential.

Inclusion, however, does not mean that all children should attend the same classroom all of the time; nor does it imply that teachers should expect to teach all children without support and accommodations. To be effective inclusive education requires appropriate time and resources. Special-needs learners are those for whom accommodations and/or modifications[1] have to be made to parts of their program. The adaptations may include how the pupil is taught, what the pupil is taught, or how the pupil is assessed.

Sometimes accommodations or modifications are only necessary for a short time, such as in the situation of someone taking notes, or scribing for a child with a broken arm. In other cases, educators must provide accommodations or modifications over the student's entire academic career. As we shall see, accommodation and modification can take a number of forms, including the use of technology. Whenever possible, however, teachers should be encouraging all pupils to learn as independently as is possible. Therefore, in cases where modifications might be necessary some of the time, teachers should ensure that when they are not, special-needs learners develop self-reliance. A suitable guide for making decisions in this regard is to provide the minimum amount of support to empower success.

Teachers new to today's inclusive classrooms must acquire knowledge of and practice in using strategies that assist special-needs learners (see Figure 9.1). New, and sometimes even experienced, teachers find this list somewhat overwhelming.

FIGURE 9.1: Some of the Special Needs in Today's Inclusive Classrooms

Special need	Characteristics which may be observed in class
Attention deficit disorder (ADD)	Serious difficulties with attention span. Often restless and is easily distracted. Has difficulty waiting turn, following instructions, and playing quietly. Does not seem to listen.
Gifted and talented	Identified as capable of high performance; demonstrates creative or productive thinking; may become bored with regular work; and may be very intense.
Hearing impairment	Frequently requests repetition, seems confused, or misses key ideas. Abnormal voice quality, which is often too loud or too soft, and with poor articulation.
Learning disabilities	Displays difficulty with listening, speaking, reading, writing, spelling, or calculating. Difficulty memorizing and reasoning abstractly.
Mental disability	Sometimes referred to as developmentally delayed. Exhibits significantly impaired functioning on most educational or skill-based activities.
Orthopaedic disabilities	Mobility or stamina problems can result from a congenital anomaly, (e.g., absence of a body part); disease, (e.g., bone tuberculosis); or other causes, (e.g., cerebral palsy). Students are often referred to as physically challenged.
Social and emotional disorders	Unable to maintain satisfactory interpersonal relationships due to aggressive, destructive, disobedient or disruptive behaviour. Minimal patience.
Visual impairment	Squints frequently and complains of blurred vision. Frequently guesses when reading. Tends to rub eyes, which are often swollen, red or watery.

How can new teachers' concerns be alleviated enough to enable them to cope with the many diversities they will meet during their early years? The teacher educator should be aware that many novices expect to be equipped with *recipes* they can use to address learners' special needs. This notion of recipe can be used as an analogy to advance the theory that different understandings and interpretations of a recipe lead to different products in different contexts—some of which are successful, some are not. It is futile to search for *blind* strategies, *deaf* skills, or *gifted* resources. Teachers have to develop techniques that work for them and their pupils, in their particular context, rather than search for the perfect lesson plan for teaching a visually impaired child how to add fractions. "Because there is no one clearly superior way to engage in educating children, teachers must constantly set hypotheses and test them, searching for the best way to teach each individual child and group of children" (Schoonmaker, 1998, p. 568).

Such an approach, however, is somewhat unnerving, not only for novice teachers, but also for some teacher educators. To develop appropriate strategies, a teacher needs to understand why particular strategies are successful and appropriate under certain circumstances and not under others; this reflective approach is an essential part of a teacher's long term growth and development. The following sections explore issues associated with teaching pupils with special needs and provide opportunities to discuss various strategies to use in different contexts with diverse pupils.

LEARNING STYLES OF DIVERSE LEARNERS

Sometimes the accommodations developed for special-needs learners have a positive impact on learning on other pupils because members of each group share similar learning styles. All pupils have preferred learning styles and the options are wide. Some pupils are auditory learners, others more visual, yet others tend to be tactile. While some learners are impulsive, others are reflective. Some view situations holistically and others analytically.

Gardner (1993) has suggested that learners also have various *intelligences*, for example, linguistic, visual/spatial, musical, bodily/kinaesthetic, intrapersonal, interpersonal, and logical/mathematical. These intelligences influence the ways in which learners *come to know* or understand a particular piece of knowledge. In order to reach as many pupils as possible, teachers must attempt to understand the preferred learning modes of their special-needs learners, and whenever feasible reframe an expectation to correspond to the learner's most suitable style of learning or intelligence. This multimodal approach often benefits more than the special-needs learners. Fasano and Brown (1992) found that secondary teachers were surprised when multimodal approaches which they had specifically designed for their special-needs learners were also effective for those considered *average* or *typical*. As mentioned, some aspects of the preferred learning styles of their *average* pupils were being dealt with successfully through this approach. Good teaching for special-needs learners is often good pedagogy for all pupils.

STRATEGIES TO ASSIST NEW TEACHERS

A flexible approach, and a commitment to provide individualized attention to all learners some of the time, are key factors when attempting to meet the needs of as many pupils as possible. It is impossible for all pupils to derive the same benefits from even the simplest lesson.

Pupils construct understanding based on numerous factors, the most significant being prior experiences. (See *Teaching From a Constructivist Views* in Chapter 2.) Since these experiences differ for each learner regardless of special needs, teachers should probably focus on helping individual pupils understand specific concepts and skills rather than attempting to teach a prescribed curriculum to them all. We have to expect different outcomes even when we start with similar expectations for everyone.

Many special-needs learners will have been placed on an Individualized Education Plan (IEP) following a meeting with teachers, parents, school administrators, and often, other necessary support personnel. Modifications may need to be made to learning sequences to maintain the focus of the IEP and to emphasize access to opportunity for the pupil. Assessment strategies that enable pupils to demonstrate their understanding in a safe environment are an essential part of the IEP. Brown and Fasano (1996) discuss the importance of both organizational and pedagogical strategies in conjunction with the IEP, when examining the inclusive classroom.

One of the organizational strategies teachers have to consider is the physical setting. Where should Angharad sit to compensate for the severe hearing loss in her left ear? What about Jason who has lost his right eye? What is the best location for Katie, who is easily distracted by those around her, and for Naveed who must manoeuvre his wheelchair? Having routines and structure for pupils with ADD and for those with severe behavioural problems is essential, as is having a few consequential, but well-established rules and procedures for everyone in the class. The cooperating teacher must model and discuss these rules and organizational structures. Student teachers not only have to *see* the theory applied during their practicum, but must also have opportunities to consult and consider *why* teachers do what they do.

Novice teachers also need to know they are not alone and learn how to access and use personnel to support the inclusive classroom. The principal or resource room teacher, in collaboration with the cooperating teacher, should discuss how the school has organized and implemented teacher support. Understanding how to contact outside specialists as well as capitalize on the available resources within a school environment, such as parent and pupil volunteers, is indispensable knowledge.

BUILDING LEARNING COMMUNITIES THAT CELEBRATE DIVERSITY

The teacher is the most influential role model for conveying respect. If teachers do not value all learners, regardless of their special needs, there is little likelihood of the classroom being a positive environment. Novice teachers need to discuss aspects of teacher behaviour that convey bias and lack of sensitivity, as well as observe models of positive values and attitudes. When teachers show they do not accept other adults or pupils in the school from whom they differ (e.g., those with an another sexual orientation or religious belief) they model an attitude incompatible with inclusion.

Establishing an environment in which all learners feel welcomed and valued takes time and effort. Building a community of learners where everyone understands why they have responsibilities as well as privileges takes a caring, thoughtful person. At the same time, even when cooperating teachers can model the conditions that epitomize inclusion, they need to discuss their attitude explicitly with student teachers. Likewise, student teachers have to do far more than passively observe the teaching and learning. They need to reflect actively on what is happening. Recording in a daily log or journal the strategies and routines used and why certain ones facilitate a safe learning milieu is important. Working in an inclusive classroom is best handled, says Schoonmaker, by those "who enjoy reaching out into the unpredictable world created by the diversity and uniqueness of each child and each group of children" (1999, p. 568).

Multimodal Approaches

While some pedagogical strategies are more useful than others for certain learning modalities, as was discussed in a previous section, they are best used together (i.e., multimodally). Visual supports, for example, are particularly important for pupils having difficulty with their reading; however, they should always be used with appropriate vocabulary. Text with enlarged print as well as rewritten texts using simplified vocabulary expedites the learning. Audio support can include tapes played in conjunction with the text, together with the discussion of fundamental details. Tactile learners need to be able to touch objects to assist their comprehension. For example, when these children learn to write letters, running a finger over a sandpaper replica will support the impact of seeing the image they have. Similarly, manipulative materials, such as base ten blocks in mathematics, benefit the tactile learner's understanding of place value. We must remember, however, that physically exploring the attributes of a concrete object takes longer for the visually impaired child and is more demanding than simply inspecting the same article visually.

Technological Approaches

Technological supports (e.g., word prediction devices) offer assistance in vocabulary and writing. Technology can assist in individualizing instruction and offers teachers many support possibilities in providing for their pupils' academic development as well as accommodating physical disabilities. Examples include predictive dictionaries or computers with larger key boards. Voice synthesizers can greatly benefit children who are visually or physically impaired. Calculators assist children who cannot remember their basic facts. Other adaptations to technological equipment, such as large keypads, help children who are physically challenged to communicate their thoughts in writing. Occupational and physical therapists often have inexpensive solutions.

Building on Success

Understanding modalities helps teachers to build on a child's strengths and to find meaningful strategies to address deficiencies. Learning-disabled children may be hindered by a poor ability to speak, perceive, think abstractly, read, write, spell, or calculate. To act appropriately a teacher must discern the traits and gravity of the disability, such as an inability to memorize or a tendency to make consistent reversals, and then help the child to adopt supportive tactics. By carefully listening to children's explanations and observing their work habits, new teachers will begin to understand students' successful thinking processes and preferred modalities for learning. Novice teachers must learn to build on success, realize that improvement usually happens slowly, and seek support outside the classroom.

Providing Structure

Providing children who have social and/or emotional disorders with structure is often key, as is reinforcing it with attainable goals and rewards. Discussing consequences for inappropriate behaviour with the child and parents and ensuring everyone understands is important. By collaborating with specialists, such as medical staff and outside agencies, teachers can learn worthwhile strategies. Consistency on the part of the teacher is imperative.

Gifted and Talented Pupils

New teachers often overlook gifted and talented pupils because, as novices, they find their many other responsibilities taxing. A number of strategies are useful. Arrange for them to interact with similar learners on a regular basis. In addition, let them mix with others so they learn to develop interaction skills for dealing with pupils not labelled as gifted. To do this, new teachers will require guidance for determining when and how to group pupils both homogeneously and heterogeneously. Discussions regarding the advantages and disadvantages of grouping styles are vital. Discussing strategies that offer challenges to gifted pupils without a major restructuring of lesson or unit plans will provide valuable support for new teachers. Enrichment activities should not simply be more of the regular classroom schedule. Gifted and talented pupils deserve material that will stretch their imagination and insight. If a teacher is using rich, open-ended tasks that have multiple solutions, then gifted pupils can often work on the same tasks as their classmates. They will, more often than not, take the task to a different level of sophistication and elegance. Alternative assessment instruments, such as rubrics, can be adopted to distinguish different levels of performance and understanding.

Assessment

All students deserve the opportunity to be successful, and assessment strategies should reveal what students know as well as what they still need to learn. Cohen and Spenciner (1998, p. 178) forewarn that it is often difficult to specify whether "... an inadequate response results from poor writing skills, poor mastery of the content, poor problem-solving skills, lack of creativity, or a combination of these factors." Teachers must develop the attitude that it is important to uncover children's strengths, rather than simply finding out what they have not yet learned.

Providing alternative assessment strategies and adjusting the time span for writing a test can counteract the anxiety many special-needs learners experience. For student teachers who have never experienced difficulties in school, reflecting on what constitutes equity, fairness, and justice is integral for their growth and development in today's inclusive classrooms. Considering alternative assessment strategies should be part of every student teacher's lesson plan and included as a central topic during post-lesson discussions.

SUPPORTING ONGOING REFLECTION AND DEVELOPMENT

Cooperating teachers can challenge a student teacher to consider alternatives by posing a simple question such as, "How might you adapt that for Jasmin?" Discussions in context are far more relevant than when hypothetical situations are presented out of context. Unless teacher educators insist that their student teachers explore alternative frameworks, they will often be overlooked. As Frances Schoonmaker explains when describing Kay, a bright and committed novice teacher:

> Like most [new] teachers, Kay is likely to become so involved in the rapidly paced life of the classroom that she will give little time to the kind of deliberation envisioned by reformers of teacher education and schools and her actions will often be inconsistent with her professional beliefs (1998, p. 561).

It is important to discuss how theory can support and inform practice, as well as understanding how practice has illuminated and developed theory. We do not learn from doing; we learn from thinking about what we have been doing. Creating a safe, welcoming environment in which new teachers can question the craft of teaching is essential if we are to move beyond simple apprenticeship. Student teachers must see exemplary educators as being those who want to grow and learn from situations that challenge us to consider alternatives if we are to find better strategies for undertaking the difficult aspects associated with our profession. Through such discussions a community is formed since:

> Those who learn from one who is still learning
> > drink from a running stream.

> Those who learn from one who has ceased to learn
> > drink from a stagnant pond. (Skemp, 1989, p. 211).

Today's inclusive classrooms are probably more diverse than ever, and change is taking place at an accelerated and unprecedented rate (Bandura, 1995). Recognizing the essential elements associated with planning for diverse learners and making accommodations within a flexible structure requires time, patience, and coaching from an experienced mentor. Teachers must determine what each student needs to be successful and make suitable accommodations. To ensure a functional inclusive classroom, they must learn to develop a safe environment where reflection and risk-taking are encouraged. What helps them do this is often their attitude toward providing for the learning needs of all students. The opportunity for making the greatest impact on them regarding inclusive classrooms happens when teachers are confronted with a real situation that has to be addressed within a limited time frame. By providing such a climate for their student teachers, cooperating teachers can best facilitate their growth and deeper consciousness. The role of the teacher educator is "not to provide answers, but to begin to develop the mental scaffold for such considerations" (Schoonmaker, 1998, p. 586). The task is demanding, and everyone will have to take some risks, face some failures, and celebrate their successes when making this ambitious and complex journey.

Can I Reach All of My Pupils?

As Alice drove into Maplegrove (pop. 987), her feelings of apprehension and exhilaration began to intensify. She had been looking forward to her first year of teaching in this small rural community for several months, but wondered what her initial appointment would be like. Alice had lived all of her life in a large metropolitan city, approximately three hours' drive from Maplegrove. She was tired of big-city living and believed a move into the country would be good for her. Her parents had often discussed their life growing up on farms, and Alice had always envied their childhood experiences. Between graduation in June and now (late August), she had travelled extensively in Europe, acquiring odd jobs so that she could see as much of the continent as possible. Now the adventure was over and Alice was ready to share her passion for literature and drama with her pupils at Grove High School.

Maplegrove was one of several small rural communities that made up the Maple Key District School Board. The primary economic base in this community was farming, and Alice had learned during her interview for the teaching position that the parents of the pupils at Grove High were hard working, conservative, religious people. Few Maple Key graduates went on to post-secondary education. Grove High was similar in composition to the other high schools in the Board, with one exception; it had built its reputation on an excellent sports program.

The principal, Stan Ireland, and the head of English, Frank Patterson, had both been raised in the area and were graduates of Grove High. Frank was presently the volleyball coach. He had inherited the position two years earlier from Stan, who was well respected in the community for having taken the boys to the provincial volleyball final in two of the five years he coached the team. Frank was hoping to emulate his predecessor's accomplishments. When Alice attended the interview, she had noticed the many athletic awards displayed in the entrance hall. She was unconcerned. Alice had enjoyed intramural sports at university and was looking forward to helping in a minor way. Her real love, however, was drama.

During her first month at Grove High Alice seldom felt accepted. Many of the local teachers had spent nearly all of their lives in the area and were suspicious of "city folk." Alice often felt alone and ignored, however, towards the end of September she made friends with a couple of women on staff and joined the community drama club. She was also given responsibility for the school drama society and was making preliminary arrangements for the annual play. Like most first-year teachers, Alice spent almost all of her evenings in her one-bedroom apartment preparing her lesson and unit plans. She was especially proud of her first-period grade 12 English preparations, and spent many hours planning interesting activities she hoped would spark the same love for the subject that she embraced. Some of the girls were responding positively, but not all pupils attended her class with enthusiasm.

Cliff Mac was the least interested in her class. Cliff was a gifted athlete, who also had a learning disability. He read at the grade 4 level, and had been diagnosed five years previously with dyslexia. Cliff's Individualized Education Plan (IEP) also indicated that he could have violent verbal outbursts directed towards his teachers and other classmates. For the first week Cliff had responded positively to Alice's teaching. She had found some appropriate reading material from her own library and attempted to involve him in the regular class activities as much as possible. He appeared to be enjoying the classes but it was obvious Cliff often felt excluded. Alice found it increasingly difficult to draw Cliff into discussions. His interest had begun to wane after those first weeks, and he was becoming less and less receptive to Alice's attempts to include him, often coming late to class. The volleyball team had practices each morning before school started, and Cliff was the best player on the team. His punctuality was questionable, but each time he was late, he had presented a written note from Mr. Patterson, the volleyball coach.

Cliff's insolence towards Alice had escalated, and for the past week Cliff and a group of his friends from the volleyball team had heckled, made faces, and whispered when other pupils made oral presentations. They were particularly cruel to the girls, especially those who were overweight or less attractive. The second time it happened Alice called Cliff to her desk and confronted him privately. He denied he was doing anything wrong, turned on his heel, and walked back to his desk. As he sat down, he muttered, just loud enough for Alice to hear, "This is only because you're jealous." Then he sat with his head on his folded arms for the rest of the class. Alice ignored him. In the following classes Cliff began mumbling, just so those around him could hear, "This class sucks, Alice clucks!" Alice could see and hear Cliff's friends chuckling, but although she thought she could hear what he had been saying, she couldn't be certain. When she challenged Cliff and spoke sternly to him about his rude behaviour, he responded curtly, "You're just picking on me because you don't like me and you think I'm dumb." Mr. Patterson, her department head, was very busy coaching and seemed to expect his department to look after their own discipline problems, yet Alice knew she couldn't allow Cliff to continue in this manner. That night Alice didn't sleep very well.

The next day, Alice divided the class into groups of three. It was the day before a decisive volleyball game, and Alice had determined that a good topic for discussion and debate would be sportsmanship and respect for teammates. She hoped that this context was one Cliff could relate to, and that the discussion might help him to realize how damaging his actions were to the morale of other members in the class—including her. When she got to the last two pupils, one of whom was Cliff, she said, "And I'll make the third, we can work together."

"No *&%~# way I'm gonna be in a group with no damn teacher!" Cliff suddenly and loudly blurted out. The class became silent. . .

QUESTIONS

Framing, Reframing, and Exploring Solutions

1. What are some possible causes for Cliff's behaviour?
2. What are some earlier actions Alice might have taken to manage Cliff's behaviour?
3. Consider the situation from the perspectives of the different participants.
   a) Frame the situation from Alice's perspective.
   b) Reframe the situation from Cliff's perspective.
   c) Reframe the situation from one of the other participant's perspective, for example, Mr. Patterson, the department head and coach; Mr. Ireland, the principal; one of the overweight girls who had been mocked; one of Cliff's peer group; or one of Cliff's parents.

    d) What do you believe each participant will consider to be a fair, just or equitable resolution to the situation?

4. Reframe the situation using data from Figure 9.1. How might the situation have unfolded if Cliff had some other special need?

5. Contemplate other ways of reframing the case; for example, consider sexual orientation, religious beliefs, race, class, gender (you might want to read Chapter 8 prior to discussing this question).

Personal Reflections and Connections

1. What are Alice's options? What would you do immediately in response to Cliff's remark? Why?

2. What are some possible *positive* and *negative* consequences to your response?

3. If you know of a situation similar to Alice's, consider how it was handled. Are there some aspects that should perhaps have been handled differently?

4. Reflect on how you might be a positive role model for pupils when dealing with issues of ethnic sensitivity, sexuality, gender, or belief systems.

5. Consider the children that you have encountered who have been identified as special-needs pupils.
    a) Describe the abilities and behaviours of two of these pupils.
    b) How did you assist their growth and development?
    c) Did they really have special needs (e.g. is ADD just an excuse for badly behaved pupils)?

Reflections on Learning-to-Teach

1. How might the whole situation have been handled differently?
    a) Consider the pros and cons of your approach.
    b) What were the pivotal factors in helping you reach a decision?

2. Richard Lavoie suggests that, "Fair does not mean that every child gets the same treatment, but that every child gets what he or she needs." Discuss.

3. Discuss the types of behaviours exhibited by teachers that establish a positive environment in today's inclusive classrooms.

ENDNOTE

1. When *accommodations* are made for pupils with special needs, the pupils are expected to fulfill the requirements of the curriculum by using those accommodations. For example, more time is provided for a pupil to complete a test if the pupil takes a longer time to process information. However, the test is the same as for all of the other pupils. A computer with an extra large keyboard is provided for a pupil with a visual impairment or orthopaedic disability, but the expectations for that pupil are similar to those for the others.

When *modifications* are made for pupils with special needs, the curriculum is changed in such a manner that the pupils have opportunities to meet new expectations. An Individualized Education Plan (IEP) is developed specifically for the pupil, usually in consultation with the classroom teacher, parents, principal, resource room teacher, and school psychologist. Accommodations might well be included as part of the IEP.

METAPHORS OF MANAGEMENT

As she sat in her Educational Psychology class with more than a hundred other student teachers, Madhu listened intently as Dr. Smith began his lectures on classroom management. Madhu could hardly wait to be a teacher; however, she had serious concerns about her ability to keep a classroom full of adolescent students quiet and on-task. Her anxieties were compounded by stories from others about their classroom management difficulties and her sense that the most common reason beginning teachers failed was their inability to maintain a disciplined classroom. Increased media attention to issues such as deteriorating behaviour and escalating violence in schools fed her fears. Thus Madhu was poised with pen in hand and a pad full of blank paper to write down everything Dr. Smith said about the topic. She was grateful that he was addressing this topic before the first practicum; she figured that she would need all the help she could get in this particular area.

Earlier in this book, learning-to-teach was described as a complex and ongoing endeavour, even for experienced teachers. And student teachers have so many new things to which they must attend at once that they may neglect classroom management. Student teachers are typically unaware of the myriad of tasks involved in establishing and maintaining a productive learning environment for 30 pupils at the same time. Yet, many educational researchers place classroom management at the centre of the task of teaching, and concerns about it drive teachers' planning and decision-making (Doyle, 1986; Berliner, 1990). Being able to predict what actions by pupils or teachers may create problematic situations in classrooms and knowing how to manage such dilemmas are some of the keys to a novice teacher's success. Pupils' actions, reactions, and assumptions (and even misconceptions) about a subject, their abilities, and their likes and dislikes of a teacher—all make a profound impact on teaching and learning experiences, and the way in which they need to be organized. Almost all student teachers worry about their ability to manage a class successfully and novices indicate they are most concerned about classroom management (Beynon, 1997; MacDonald & Healy, 1999).

In this chapter, we discuss the complex issue of managing the modern classroom and examine how the practicum may contribute to or weaken a novice teacher's ability to master this central function. Following a brief review of the literature on classroom management, we introduce the concept of metaphor as one means of thinking about classroom organization and conclude with a case study from Madhu's experiences during student teaching. We tell it first from her perspective and then from that of her cooperating teacher.

CLASSROOM MANAGEMENT: A RESEARCH PERSPECTIVE

While beginning teachers may have internalized theories of classroom management from their pre-service program and own experience, they typically lack the complex skills needed to manage actual situations effectively (Beynon, 1994; Bullough, 1994). Frequently, tension arises when student teachers realize during the practicum that they do not understand situations that need management as well as they thought they did. There can be many reasons for this. Perhaps novice teachers tend to focus on the entire class when a student misbehaves, whereas experienced teachers tend to base strategy decisions on the individual student's performance (Housner & Griffey, 1986). Or, student teachers may have only interpreted their early experiences with classroom management practices from the perspective of a pupil and may not realize that many of the tacit practices teachers carry out have a planned effect on the learning environment. Beginning teachers tend to seek specific skills to control their students rather than develop a framework of skills congruent with their overall orientation to classroom management (Beynon, 1994). Secure in the knowledge that four years of university education has made them more mature and competent in subject content, novice teachers may see their role as one in which they must transmit their knowledge. Consequently, they focus on teaching skills that promote transmission of knowledge as opposed to those that develop an environment for learning.

What do student teachers learn about classroom management during their student teaching experiences? The answer is not at all clear. Some researchers (Feiman-Nemser & Buchmann, 1987; Johnston, 1994) argue that the practicum may actually inhibit novices from learning-to-teach. Rather, student teachers may only learn *tricks of the trade* from watching and mimicking experienced teachers. They may be socialized into copying their supervising teacher's teaching style because it worked in a particular situation, hoping that the techniques will be useful in the future. This type of learning undermines the purpose of teacher education; it tends to reduce teaching and learning to a set of technical skills, which often fail inexperienced teachers.

Others have noted that too often student teachers are given only a wide variety of theoretical views about maintaining a learning environment. This information is virtually useless unless they also learn specific, technical skills for dealing with some classroom problems (Lasley, 1994). Balance is important, and dealing with classroom management issues is yet another part of teaching that is contested and controversial, making the process of learning-to-teach even more complicated.

In order to challenge beginning teachers' preconceptions about management strategies, teacher educators must provide opportunities for them to take risks within a controlled environment and then to engage in open and frequent discussions with an experienced mentor. For example, Swanson, O'Connor, and Cooney (1990) developed a study in which they gave 24 beginning teachers and 24 experienced teachers several management incidents to ponder. They asked all of the teachers to record their thought processes out loud as they solved the various problems. Not surprisingly, they found that the expert teachers and novices solved the problems quite differently. And, they noted that while both groups demonstrated that they had sufficient knowledge and skills to solve a problem, the experienced teachers used knowledge and reflections based on past experience in similar situations. The experienced teachers had what Swanson et al. termed a "qualitative completeness" in their minds as they managed or solved management problems, something that the novices lacked. Studies such as this suggest that the reflections of expert teachers about classroom management problems as well as their actions are more thorough than are those of novice teachers. Qualitative completeness may be seen to develop as a result of the framing and reframing of problematic situations in context. We will see, in this chapter, how this action plays a crucial role in organizing and managing or solving classroom dilemmas. If the practicum is to be truly educative and productive, then student teachers must not only acquire theory and observe classroom management techniques, but also frame and reframe classroom management situations which they face.

Swanson, O'Connor, and Cooney's study complements others (e.g., Doyle, 1986; Chi, Feltovich & Glaser, 1981; Newell & Simon, 1972) that point to the different strategies beginning and experienced teachers use in managing/solving classroom management problems. Experienced teachers' prior knowledge and learning about classroom management are important because they make explicit the difference in the knowledge bases of student teachers and their cooperating teachers. Such knowledge candidly presupposes the help that an experienced cooperating teacher can provide for a student teacher in developing appropriate classroom management strategies in the context of the cooperating teacher's class. Understanding that their knowledge bases differ may enable the experienced cooperating teacher to understand why student teachers focus on different elements of behaviour. It will help cooperating teachers assist their student teachers to develop a professional conversation about alternative strategies.

Sociologists maintain that a *hidden curriculum* results from the enforcement of explicit and implicit rules of behaviour in the classroom, such as respect for authority, and the ability to sit still for long periods of time. There is a pervading but false implication that attentiveness means the material being presented is significant and that important learning must be taking place. The value of these outcomes is controversial (Posner, 1989) and a dramatic shift away from the behavioural approach to other approaches of classroom management has happened mainly because traditional ways of teaching are being replaced by more socially interactive methods which require different strategies.

Student teachers, in their uncertainty, may think they want the *recipes* to fix a variety of problematic situations in their classrooms. They tend to believe that they will learn these solutions in their preservice year. If school-based and university-based teacher educators succumb and only provide instant solutions, then beginning teachers may perceive that the expert wisdom that was provided by their teacher educators describes the only way to manage a situation. Novice teachers may feel compelled to use strategies specific to one situation over and over even though circumstances and results vary. On the other hand, if teacher educators convey the complexity of learning-to-teach and the role that classroom management plays within it, student teachers are more likely to gain a better perspective on classroom management within the teaching/learning process and its relationship to pedagogical content knowledge. Student teachers require multiple opportunities in which to practise different management strategies and time afterward with experienced practitioners to examine the qualitative completeness of their actions. Instead of equipping student teachers with a skill to handle a one-time situation, teacher educators should try to share their wisdom and reflective practice to help student teachers develop thoughtful, professional understanding of teaching, which can lead to a career-long pattern of reflection and development.

THE USE OF METAPHOR FOR PROMOTING UNDERSTANDING OF CLASSROOM MANAGEMENT

In this chapter we use the concept of metaphor to assist student teachers and teacher educators in considering and understanding classroom management. Identifying metaphors equips practitioners to explore and expand preconceptions, and to facilitate reflective processes in framing and reframing situations for managing or solving situations. A metaphor supplies us with a set of conceptual categories with which we can frame a classroom management situation (i.e., it provides conceptual language for classroom management that helps us make sense of what is going on).

In fact, the term *classroom management* is in itself a metaphor that we commonly use to portray a productive teaching environment. It conjures up images of ideal classrooms that are orderly and productive, probably fairly quiet, and portrays teachers who are in authority in that environment and pupils who are there to learn. Aside from this somewhat delimiting view, metaphors may prove helpful for student teachers like Madhu to consider when thinking about classroom management and its relationship to teaching. Recent literature notes that the images or metaphors teachers use in thinking about their practice play an influential role in how they behave and carry out their role. For example, in a recent study of student teachers' teaching, Morine-Dershimer & Reeve (1994) analyzed videotaped lessons that were deemed to be successful based on pupils' written results and responses. These lessons were compared with lessons judged to be not as successful. The researchers concluded that student teachers' concepts of classroom management varied significantly and that their unprompted use of metaphoric language seemed to reflect their tacit beliefs about teaching and learning, which influenced the level of interactivity in the learning and subsequently how they perceived classroom management. Metaphoric description of a situation seems to help student teachers learn *how* to teach rather than just learn *about* teaching.

In order to explicate the concept of metaphor in learning-to-teach, we describe two metaphors of classroom management from opposite ends of the spectrum. Consider the following metaphors that have been used to describe approaches to classroom management; try to visualize and describe the learning environment in that particular classroom.

Teacher as Dictator

We begin with the metaphor, *teacher as dictator*, one that might be remembered as a more historical outlook, reminiscent of the view of teaching as transmission (see Chapter 2).

Bullough (1994) notes that traditionally, discipline in the classroom was viewed as being analogous to organizing and supervising a labor force. Teachers were authoritative, organized, and impersonal dictators who forced students to be quiet and orderly in order to learn. This image reinforces the view of the hidden curriculum underlying situations in which students are perceived as passive learners—or empty vessels waiting to be filled with knowledge—and teachers as the deliverers of knowledge; it supports the naive view that an orderly, quiet classroom is evidence of learning. In this metaphor pupil compliance and obedience are seen as the keys to a successful classroom. The real problem with it is that current student teachers like Madhu may have been *educated* in such classrooms and believe that the only way to be successful is to have an orderly, silent classroom.

Before leaving this metaphor, it is important to acknowledge that the teacher as dictator metaphor may not reflect only an historic view. Currently, some school districts are calling emphatically for "back to the basics" in curriculum in an attempt to raise deteriorating standards. Concomitant with a back to the basics stance is authoritative discipline and control over pupils and learning. Recollections of the past always seem to radiate memories of better and simpler times.

Teacher as Negotiator

Next, we look at a metaphor of classroom management at the other end of the spectrum—that of teacher as negotiator. As one moves away from the stance of teacher in charge, the question of authority arises. Instead of having authority over pupils, these teachers see themselves as having authority of expertise and as being informed, guiding mediators who must negotiate with and share the control of the classroom with their pupils. In such a democratic environment, pupils are required to assume responsibility, self-discipline, and control of their own learning and of the learning environment. Pupils are expected to be involved in community decisions such as establishing the physical layout within the classroom, developing rules, and organizing learning activities by cooperatively determining topics within a curriculum unit. Teachers are expected to respect their pupils' needs, to trust their aspirations, and to work effectively within that environment. A trusting, cooperative relationship and mutual respect between teacher and pupil are paramount in this image.

> Negotiatory acts are a form of power sharing that represents the teachers' caring commitment to democratic governance and an exploration of alternative forms of social control (McLaughlin, 1994, p. 80).

While this view of classroom management sounds ideal, novice teachers may find it far more difficult to put into practice. Some issues must be dealt with authoritatively perhaps because certain factors (e.g., safety) may be paramount.

The literature uses a variety of metaphors in discussing classroom management, and the two described above were selected because they represent opposite ends of the spectrum. For example, the teacher as dictator likely sees teaching as transmissive and offers learning activities based on a one-size-fits-all approach. On the other hand, the teacher as negotiator expects learners to take responsibility for their own learning needs and is prepared to teach in whatever way the learner requests and rationalizes. Both metaphors provide a learning environment for both pupils and teachers (and concomitant classroom management issues), and we are not about to claim that one is better or more useful than the other. All teachers, in their professional growth, need to consider which metaphor (and which kinds of metaphors) suits them personally and professionally.

Learning-to-Teach as a Technician

Some writers believe that novice teachers do better by taking intermediate steps before settling on particular ways of managing classrooms. Lasley (1994) posits an intermediate stage of metaphoric development. The technical or skill-based teacher is perhaps a more controversial metaphor but it allows novice teachers to experiment in an intermediary phase to practise their competence. Lasley believes that student teachers should learn a limited number of teaching skills (i.e., three) for the purposes of classroom management, practice those skills under guidance, and receive feedback on their use of them. Lasley's thesis is that once student teachers have practised, had feedback about, and mastered those three skills, they will have developed the confidence to adapt their knowledge and skill level when developing and practising different management skills, and will be able to move quite naturally beyond the merely technical level. While the strengths of this metaphor seem obvious, earlier comments in this chapter indicate that this approach may actually encourage novice teachers to seek out *recipes* to solve problems, so we worry that such an approach may inhibit their quest to find the best methods.

Figure 10.1 provides a partial list of other metaphors you can use to explore management options. Use it to consider the images of teaching and classrooms that they bring to mind. Like those described earlier, each of these metaphors favours a particular emphasis in teaching and views good teaching in a unique way.

We introduced two disparate metaphors in this chapter that can be used for framing and reframing classroom management situations. Realistically, however, it would be naive to assume that a one-metaphor-fits-all approach exists; teaching is far more complex than that. Metaphors must be framed and reframed as situations and circumstances change, as teacher and pupil personalities interact, and as intent, dynamics, and shape develop.

Sometimes we discover incongruities between what we think we must do and say as teachers and how we feel we should act. Tensions develop as personal, physical, and internal conflicts arise and leave us with a problem to solve, or more likely, a dilemma to

---

FIGURE 10.1: Metaphors for Management

Think about each of the following metaphors for management carefully. Consider the role of the teacher in the classroom and of the pupil, and the curriculum and the organization of physical space. Identify which images appeal or do not appeal to you as a teacher and the reasons for that. What inferences about teaching does each of the follow bring to mind?

- teacher as reflective practitioner (Zeichner & Liston, 1987)
- teacher as executive (Berliner, 1990)
- teacher as protector or as prison guard (Weinstein, Woolfolk, Dittmeier, Shanker, 1994)
- teacher as recreation director

manage. Nonetheless, considering metaphors can be an effective strategy for novice teachers to use to explore their tacit views of themselves as teachers and to flesh out their underlying beliefs of teaching. Metaphors allow teachers to look inwardly and to begin to understand how their own personal nature affects, or even biases, their views of learning, classroom organization, and even how they regard others. However, during this process of inner reflection, novice teachers may find that, while they tend to gravitate toward one end of the continuum in their personal and professional views, they find tension in acting that way as a teacher. Instead of asking themselves, *What kind of teacher can I be?* they may well find themselves asking, *What kind of teacher do I have to be in this situation?* or *What kind of teacher am I predisposed to be?*

SUMMARY AND CONCLUSIONS

In the practicum classroom, the metaphors, routines, and idiosyncrasies of their cooperating teachers influence student teachers; the overt and implicit practices and metaphors of their university instructors may also sway them. At the same time, they are influenced by their own predispositions and backgrounds, and cannot ignore their predilections. Simultaneously, student teachers are dealing with the varied images of their elementary and secondary schools teachers, while negotiating their own views. No wonder the topic of classroom management is both frightening and confusing. In the meantime, student teachers are left in a dilemma of trying to develop an active, stimulating learning environment while maintaining control over their students in borrowed classrooms. Because learning-to-teach is so complex, even murky, the consideration of classroom management, to be most useful to teacher learners (whether novice or experienced), needs to be carefully considered, then framed and reframed, or metamorphosed, as situations change or develop.

Give the Student Teacher a Hand

From the Student Teacher's Perspective

Like most student teachers in their first practicum setting, Madhu was a bit nervous about her ability to make the transition from student to teacher. She was assigned to a primarily homogeneous, white, middle-class suburban public school to teach grade 7 and 8 music. Her undergraduate degree was in Music, with an area of specialization in vocal and choral pedagogy. Her placement, however, was with a cooperating teacher who specialized in instrumental music and taught intermediate students. This added to Madhu's nervousness about her placement. Madhu worried about her lack of knowledge of instrumental music and its effect on her ability to manage the various classes. For example, she wondered: What if they ask me how to play a note and I don't know the fingering? They'll know that I don't know anything about teaching band, and I will lose control.

Madhu's worries were amplified as she learned more about her placement. Her cooperating teacher, John, had a reputation in the educational community as an outstanding teacher. A little daunted by his reputation, she found him to be a quiet, reserved man, who seemed supportive and reassuring as he worked with her in the practicum. This calm support helped Madhu to feel a growing confidence in her ability to conduct the instrumental classes.

Most of the classes went relatively smoothly under the influence of the cooperating teacher's presence. However, if John left the room, even for a few minutes to retrieve something from his adjoining office, the class dynamics immediately transformed, and Madhu would find herself faced with 30 adolescents who seemed to know she was a novice. Classroom management difficulties occurred quickly. The students began talking to each other and she would spend several minutes settling them down. The only way to keep them under control was literally to keep their instruments in their mouths.

On Friday afternoon, after a week at the school, Madhu was in front of the classroom teaching a class of grade 8 instrumental students. It was her first time teaching them but she had observed these students and participated in co-teaching them each day throughout the past week. John was walking around the room helping students here and there for most of the period and Madhu felt the class was going well. John just sat down to make some notes for their conference afterward when they heard a knock at the closed door. It was the principal asking John if he could speak to him for a moment. John must have felt confident that Madhu could teach by herself if given the opportunity because he stepped into the hall, shutting the door behind him. At the sound of the closing door, the or-

derly and respectful students changed; there were toots and honks erupting around the room from the instruments. Other students began talking and making smart remarks to her. However, Madhu was determined to continue with the lesson, and in so doing, hoped to keep the students under control. Her mind raced as she began to think of all the techniques she knew to settle the students down again and to continue with her lesson plan.

As Madhu struggled to manage the rebellious musicians, a trombone player at the back of the room slowly turned her music stand around to face Madhu. On the stand lay a human hand! It was autumn, and Madhu immediately assumed this was a Halloween prank. As she turned to speak to the student, however, she noticed a bloody stump at the end of the girl's arm. Madhu's knees felt weak, the blood drained from her face, and an eerie quiet filled the room. All the students stared at her, intently waiting for her reaction. Just then the door opened and John walked back into the class. The girl immediately turned the music stand around and promptly reattached her prosthesis. The students' posture was perfect as they appeared to be obediently enraptured with Madhu's every word. Madhu's first reaction was relief at being rescued from dealing with the situation. Her next was anger. She was angry with the cooperating teacher for leaving her alone with the class and for not informing her about the girl with the prosthesis.

When she told him what had happened, John found the incident fairly humorous (which made Madhu even more upset), and reacted by saying "I left you for five minutes because I was called away by the principal. I thought that this would give you an idea of what it's really like teaching on your own. What will you do when you have your own classes?" He also told her that after being in the classroom for the last few days, he thought that Madhu would have noticed the trombone player with the artificial hand.

Madhu was upset with John's response to this incident. She felt that the students knew they had succeeded in ruining her class and she worried about her ability to handle classroom management on her own. She left the school that day feeling frustrated, angry, and quite anxious. What if John assigned this class to her again? How would she manage this class on her own again, especially if he left the room?

From the Cooperating Teacher's Perspective

John had been teaching instrumental music to the grade 7 and 8 students at Southwinds Elementary School for the past two years. A young, enthusiastic teacher, he found Southwinds to be a suburban public school in a neighbourhood that had been a stable microcosm of middle class values for the past 20 or 30 years. At this point, the community was beginning to experience radical change as more and more multi-family subsidized housing began to fill the few green spaces in the area and the student population began to reflect some of the diversity in race and class of the larger multicultural community. He wondered how this change in demography should impact his teaching practice. Staff meetings were devoted more and more to addressing the needs of diverse learners. For the most part the students were responsive to the music program; however, support seemed to be diminishing for arts programs in the educational system.

John knew that many of his colleagues in other district schools were fighting to save arts programs and found he spent as much time advocating for strong arts programs as he did in planning his teaching. He poured most of his energy into his career and spent long hours organizing and preparing a solid curriculum. After only five years of experience, he was already recognized in the music education community as a dedicated and excellent teacher. Because of his competence, John was asked by his principal to take student teachers from the local teacher education institution. When he expressed a concern as to what he should do, his principal recommended, "Just teach them the way you were taught; treat them the way you were treated. You'll do a fine job. We want more teachers like you in the system." Although he was reluctant, John agreed.

In his first year as a cooperating teacher, John found he enjoyed working with the student teachers. They were close to his age and seemed to share many of the same interests. The faculty advisor with whom he worked was the same person who had instructed him at the Faculty of Education, and John felt reasonably comfortable. He was a cooperating teacher who tried to provide ongoing and conscientious feedback to his student teachers. He did not give them a lot of praise but the faculty advisor told him that he seemed to be quite insightful in helping his student teachers learn and improve.

Madhu was his fifth student teacher. Although she seemed quite confident, she had expressed concern about her lack of background knowledge in instrumental music. She was a vocal major and had only a passing knowledge of teaching in the wind class. Given the busyness of his day-to-day responsibilities, John was somewhat annoyed that the Faculty of Education would send him someone with so little academic background for his classroom and he certainly did not need to help someone learn both the subject matter and how to teach it in four short weeks. Nevertheless, he tried to assure Madhu that she should not worry and gave her some hints so the students would not be aware of her limited background.

During the first week, he taught while she observed and then coached various pupils individually in the room. He thought that if she had an opportunity to move among the pupils in the classroom, helping here and there, she would learn the subject matter and gain some confidence in herself. During the week he felt that although Madhu seemed shy and hesitant as a teacher, she had responded well to his suggestions, had worked hard, and acted upon all recommendations, and it was time for her to practise on her own. At the end of the first week, John told her that he felt she was ready to try to teach a 40-minute class and assigned a particular grade 8 class to her because, although he always had to work hard to keep them on task, he found them to be the most well-behaved of his classes. He told her he would move about the room to coach the students while she was teaching. John assured her that if there were a problem, such as a question about an unknown fingering or a problem with an instrument, he would deal with it quietly at the back. John told Madhu just to focus on organizing her lesson around the learning expectations they had discussed and then to teach as confidently as she could. He

was somewhat worried about how she would do and hoped that her shy demeanour would blossom into a more sparkling teacher persona when she got up in front of the class.

The class proceeded as he had expected. Madhu plodded through her lesson plan while John walked about the class focusing attention here, glaring at a recalcitrant student there, and generally trying to help her through this first lesson. He heard the mutterings from some students about how boring she was or what a waste of time this class was, and he stopped to work individually with pupils in an attempt to stem the flow of criticism. About ten minutes before the end of the class, the principal came to the door of the room and motioned to John. John could see that Madhu seemed oblivious to the pacing of the lesson and the feelings of the pupils, and her eyes and voice indicated she was trying to keep things going until the bell would ring. However, thinking things were relatively stable, John stepped outside the door with the principal for a few moments. When he re-entered the room, John noticed that Madhu looked a little more flustered than when he left but he also saw that the students were quiet, orderly and waiting to play. Nothing seemed amiss and he was impressed and relieved that Madhu had handled the situation on her own, even if it was only for a few moments. He helped Madhu end the class and made a mental note to compliment her on her teaching and her control of the students. John was sure that Madhu would be pleased with the outcome of this lesson and would gain some more confidence in herself as a teacher.

After all of the students were gone, John was just ready to compliment her work when Madhu turned to him, on the point of tears, and told him of the incident with the girl with the prosthesis. She was politely upset with him for not telling her about the girl's disability. John found the description of the event fairly humorous himself (which made Madhu even more upset), and he reacted by saying "I left you for five minutes because I was called away by the principal. I thought that this would give you an idea of what it's really like teaching on your own. What will you do when you have your own classes?" He also told her that after being in the classroom for the last five days, he thought that Madhu would have noticed the trombone player with the artificial hand because she frequently had to adjust it as she played.

It was the end of a long week, and John told Madhu to forget about it. He tried to divert her attention by planning the agenda for the next few days with her. After their conference, he decided he would talk to the pupil in the next class to hear her side of the story. Having endured his own tenure as a student and beginning teacher, he knew that Madhu had a long way to go and that she would have to learn how to work with students so that they would not misbehave. He also remembered what it was like to try to control someone else's class and knew that it was always tough. He wondered if it was wise to leave student teachers on their own for a few minutes at a time so they could feel what it was like to be the teacher-in-charge. Yet, as a new teacher himself, John had to continually work at keeping his pupils on task. Even this class caused him to focus all his energies on organization and pacing so that the pupils would not have time to socialize or disrupt things. At the same time John also felt encouraged about his own work although he felt a little guilty about it. His students obviously respected him enough to change their behaviour as soon as he re-entered the room, and he was surprised that the pupils had done that because they certainly were not always that well behaved for him. He too had to work continuously at managing a productive learning environment.

QUESTIONS

Framing, Reframing, and Exploring Solutions:

1. Consider how Madhu framed this situation and then how John framed it. Try to establish the similarities and differences in their views, considering why their views and reactions to the situation were so different.

2. If Madhu had chosen a metaphor of teacher as dictator to solve her dilemma in the class, what actions might she have taken? What if she had chosen to be a negotiatory teacher? What actions would she have taken? Which do you think would be more effective?

3. Could Madhu have prevented this incident from happening? What strategies could she have used to restore order to her classroom if John had not returned?

4. Should John have told Madhu about the girl with the prosthesis? Why or why not? Should he have left Madhu alone with the class? Why or why not?

5. Reframe the situation from a faculty advisor's perspective—dropping in on the conversation after school on Friday.

Personal Reflections and Connections

1. If you were in Madhu's position, would you have discussed the incident with anyone? Why or why not, and if so, with whom? Have you ever been in a teaching situation where you felt that your ability to manage the classroom was compromised? Describe the situation and how you dealt with it.

2. As Madhu's cooperating teacher, how would you have discussed the situation to assist her professional and personal growth?

3. Think of a metaphor that describes Madhu's situation as portrayed in this case study.

4. Describe a learning environment and what classroom management means to you.

Reflections on Learning-to-Teach

1. Classroom management issues are usually more complex than they appear on the surface. What strategies do you use to manage the problems that occur in class? How can you teach someone else what you know about classroom management without resorting to a series of how-to's?

2. If the teacher in authority (in this case, the cooperating teacher) is always in the room when a student teacher is teaching, can student teachers become *authors* of their own experience? How?

3. Choose two of the following metaphors and describe what they mean in relation to organizing a learning environment: teacher as manager, teacher as prison guard, teacher as comedian, teacher as reflective practitioner.

4. Describe your metaphor of teaching. What are its advantages? What are its weaknesses?

5. The chapter began with Madhu waiting attentively and anxiously in her Educational Psychology class to learn about classroom management. The chapter ended with a case study in which Madhu's worst fears turn to reality: she is faced with a management dilemma. What strategies can teacher educators in universities and schools use to link the learning about teaching in both situations?

6. Are there specific skills, formulae, and/or strategies for controlling student behaviour that student teachers should be taught and expected to practise in their student teaching? If so, what are they?

EVALUATING STUDENT TEACHERS: MENTOR OR GATEKEEPER?

For cooperating teachers the task of evaluating[1] student teachers, as Berard (1988) has noted, is more controversial, problematic, and stressful than any other aspect of their job (p. 210). Cooperating teachers are given two distinct and complex roles when asked to supervise and evaluate student teachers, and in many respects these roles conflict with each other. One fundamental role is that of *mentor*. Recognizing and building on a new teacher's natural strengths, diagnosing weaknesses that need to be improved, and discussing the uncountable characteristics that are part of good pedagogy, requires a mentor who has thought deeply about teaching and learning. Such mentors understand teaching as a lifetime's journey that is just beginning with the practicum. They recognize that even though student teachers have to weather their early years of teaching, they also require appropriate strategies for growth and development over the longer period. The cooperating teacher's second role is that of *gatekeeper*, charged with the responsibility of insuring that those who are unsuitable do not enter the profession.

Accommodating the conflicting roles of mentor and gatekeeper creates tensions for most cooperating teachers. While some might propose that these two roles—mentor and gatekeeper—should be separated, we do not believe this separation is advisable and instead suggest we need to frame the tensions of the two roles as a dilemma that will have to be managed (see Chapter 4). How can one be seen as a student teacher's guide and confidant, while at the same time determining that person's future? In this chapter we discuss these tensions and offer suggestions for managing the underlying dilemma. We will also consider approaches that supervisors and student teachers can use in their search to understand how one learns to teach. And we will describe why we believe that cooperating teachers have to continue in their dual roles providing guidance and encouragement while at the same time determining who should, and should not, enter the profession.

Prior to exploring these issues, however, we turn to what is perhaps a teacher educator's most important responsibility, giving novices information about their teaching that makes sense and assists them to grow and develop.

PROVIDING FEEDBACK

Since change has to come from within, student teachers need to receive and learn to internalize feedback if they are to change over the long term and not merely conform in order to receive a good final evaluation. To be effective, it is important for everyone to view the data in the feedback from their own point of view as well as from that of the other practicum participants. Beginning to understand the beliefs, fears, and predispositions of the other participants is a fundamental prerequisite for shared information to be useful (see Chapter 7).

Typically, the practicum is the only time in their career when teachers have another knowledgeable professional focus on them on a daily basis in order to provide ongoing feedback. To make the best use of the opportunity it is essential to give student teachers credible, consistent, specific, and understandable feedback. It is also vital for them to reflect on their own lessons prior to receiving feedback because they have to learn how to critique their own teaching if they are to grow professionally. Listening to student teachers analyze their lessons, describing strategies that they thought were worthwhile, as well as identifying areas needing improvement, is a vital aspect of the teacher educator's role during teaching conferences in helping student teachers to develop the expertise to critique themselves well.

When student teachers leave the supportive environment of their cooperating teachers' classrooms, they should have sufficiently refined their self-evaluation skills to begin their careers as autonomous practitioners. Ideas and strategies they have articulated explicitly have a greater likelihood of being incorporated into their teaching repertoires than do strategies they did not fully elucidate. Novice teachers need to reflect on those occasions when their teaching styles confirm or contradict their philosophy on learning.

Helping student teachers develop defensible, productive self-evaluation strategies that can be used throughout their careers is probably the most important contribution that teacher educators can make to novices' long-term growth. Teachers who learn to regularly reflect on their own practice in a critical, thoughtful manner have the means to continue to progress. Ideally, the journey of reflective practice begins as early as the first practicum

Pre-Teaching Conferences

Finding the time to discuss teaching strategies and offer feedback is imperative for a new teacher's development. Arranging pre-teaching conferences is essential for two reasons. They provide an opportunity for student teachers to explain their lesson and let the mentor discuss or question vital features prior to the lesson. A variety of aspects need to be considered to accomplish a productive pre-teaching conference. Among these are

- establishing a positive, trusting student teacher/teacher educator relationship (see Chapter 7)

- cultivating discussions concerning the strengths of the student teacher's planning, as well as diagnosing components of the lesson which need revision

- clarifying the teaching and assessment strategies for the lesson to be observed

While a variety of approaches can accomplish this last task, some questions cooperating teachers might ask or student teachers might reflect on are

- What are you/am I attempting to accomplish?

- What prior knowledge do your/my pupils need to be successful?

- Why have you/I selected specific materials/activities/investigations?

- How will you/I know if the children have learned what you/I expected them to learn?

- Are there some children for whom you/I will have to make modifications or accommodations?

Post-Teaching Conference

During the teaching session, teacher educators and student teachers need to collect data to use during the post-teaching conference. The post-teaching conference should take place in private, and allow for an exchange of opinions and ideas. Both written and oral feedback need to be provided so student teachers have a chance to reflect on the information by themselves, when they feel less stress. Learning to communicate this information in a positive and honest manner is a skill that improves with experience. Some goals to consider when discussing the teaching with the student teacher are

- making the conference participatory. Prior to discussing the lesson, student teachers should be asked to identify two or three aspects of the teaching experience they believe were successful. Student teachers have to be able to identify qualities that contribute to their effectiveness if they are to build these features into future lessons. They should then be asked to identify two or three aspects that need improvement. Finally, teacher educators should share their perspectives. The focus should be on the strengths and dealing with weaknesses in relation to the strengths.

- presenting feedback in a way that will stimulate insights and further a desire to become involved in the learning process.

- helping and encouraging student teachers to move towards professional independence.

- when necessary, leaving student teachers with a clear understanding concerning directions for change.

- asking student teachers to review what they believe they have heard.

Teaching conferences should occur on a daily basis so that student teachers, together with their teacher educators, can reflect consistently on the practicum. Because it is essential for student teachers to develop their self-evaluation skills, teacher educators have to develop strategies which assist their student teachers in becoming reflective evaluators of their own teaching and the pupils' learning. Finding the time for daily conferences and opening channels of communication are both difficult, and there never seems to be enough time to achieve everything one hopes to accomplish. Therefore, it is important to build opportunities for providing feedback into the overall structure of the supervisory process.

ASSISTING GROWTH: THE ROLE OF MENTOR

While critiquing a teacher's practice and evaluating a teacher's competence will never be a pure science, in this section we discuss various approaches for collecting quantitative and qualitative information. We suggest how each of the approaches might be employed profitably and mention some limitations. As a word of caution, many methods for measuring a teacher's effectiveness, for example, classroom observations, self-evaluation, and peer evaluation, often have low levels of reliability, validity, or generalizability (Lewis, 1982; Peterson & Kauchak, 1982). Because of the developmental nature of learning to teach and the complexity of the task, all participants need a variety of methods for collecting data on a range of skills, knowledge, values, and dispositions. And context always has to be taken into account. Maintaining an open mind while using multiple approaches is perhaps the best advice we can offer. Communication among cooperating teacher, student teacher, and faculty advisor is vital if all participants are to believe that a fair process has taken place. Consequently, no one approach should be used in isolation.

Formative evaluation is the technical term for the continual feedback mentors provide. It focuses on the ongoing work related to teaching that a student teacher carries out. Frequent, informative feedback assists the student teacher in reflecting on the process and in making adjustments accordingly. Cooperating teachers need to record their observations, comments, and reflections. By the end of a practicum, this record provides an account of issues encountered and discussed. The information also offers student teachers an ongoing account of their professional performance and presents opportunities to establish and maintain clear and open lines of communication. The following approaches are suitable methods for assisting discussion and facilitating reflection-on-action (see Chapter 3).

Video Taping

Video taping allows mentors and student teachers to replay teaching episodes. The camera catches actions of which student teachers might be totally unaware and provides data for analysis with and without their supervisors. After reviewing a segment, student teachers can discuss specific incidents or reflect on them alone. The process may enable them to consciously incorporate exemplary strategies into future lessons. Replaying segments allows the novice, with the assistance of the mentor, to reframe situations so as to explore alternative courses of action. Keep in mind, however, that the camera only replays part of the action in the learning environment; it is blind to areas outside its range of view. As well, remember that first attempts at video taping may not be successful. Both pupils and student teachers have to become comfortable with the intrusive nature of the camera. Also, the process may have to be arranged well in advance if the school district requires that parental permission be obtained prior to taping.

Peer Evaluation

By asking peers to evaluate their teaching, student teachers invite opportunities to hear perspectives from non-threatening sources. Receiving feedback from a variety of sources often helps to clarify critical situations. Although peers may not have the pedagogical expertise of the cooperating teacher or faculty advisor, that does not imply that they cannot offer advice as well as support to other student teachers. In fact, the peer is often at a similar stage of development and so has kindred concerns.

Characteristics to be evaluated should be determined by the student teacher being critiqued and discussed with the observing peer prior to the lesson. Peers can often collect data that are easily observable and relatively objective, for example, quantity of interactions with certain individuals or groups, types of questions asked, behaviours of individual pupils in the class, or classroom management techniques. Judgments that require greater pedagogical expertise on the part of the observer should generally remain the responsibility of the cooperating teacher or faculty advisor. Nevertheless, peers who are experiencing similar concerns to those of their fellow student teacher can sometimes communicate in a manner unavailable to the teacher educator, thereby explaining a situation that might otherwise remain unresolved.

Journals

Keeping journals enables student teachers to record their experiences and reflections and encourages self-evaluation. Student teachers frequently use them to reflect on pivotal teaching and learning episodes. Occasionally, student teachers and their supervisors use the journal as a vehicle for further consideration of incidents that are important for them. Such records are called response journals and are most often kept when student teachers and teacher educators wish to consider their responses over an extended time frame before discussing the situation. Journals should only be used when both the student teacher and teacher educator are comfortable with this form of communication. Many find response journals time consuming. Yet, for those who enjoy reflecting on their life through writing, response or personal journals can be extremely rewarding.

Logbooks

Logbooks, as opposed to journals, are repositories for artifacts collected from instances of teaching. They typically contain copies of lesson plans, written feedback, handouts, selected pupil work, etc. Logbooks enable student teachers to compile a record of their experiences during the practicum. They should encourage reflection, but tend not to be as detailed or personal as journals, and generally encompass a more expansive format. The logbook may be kept in a binder that is separated into components, e.g., learning environment, teacher observations, pupils, classroom management, and assessment strategies, which student teachers should attend to and reflect on during the practicum. Some use the logbook basically as a *filing cabinet* from which artifacts for the portfolio (discussed in the next section) are selected.

Portfolios

Portfolios, collections of artifacts and explanations, equip student teachers with a means to communicate qualities they consider important in their development and provide an excellent basis for reflection and discussion. The portfolio should contain a collection of artifacts that confirm evidence of professional understanding and growth, and each item should be briefly explained by the student teacher in a critical, thoughtful manner to indicate why it has been included.

Portfolios can also assist novices in securing employment and future employers in hiring suitable staff members. Montgomery (1997) suggests prospective employers are looking for evidence of the following competencies: planning skills, classroom management philosophy, reflective abilities, knowledge of appropriate assessment strategies, and the initiative to do more than is expected. Consequently, the portfolio should consist of sections that provide evidence of each of these competencies. In a survey of school administrators, Newman, Smolen and Newman (cited in Montgomery, 1997, p. 217) found that 48 per cent of the 65 administrators surveyed spent between three and ten minutes reading a student teacher's portfolio. Hence, the essential components need to be highlighted in a brief summary, with evidence provided in an appendix.

Checklists

A checklist of expected behaviours has the advantage of being easy to read by the student teacher and, for the most part, easy to complete by the cooperating teacher or faculty advisor. Student teachers can quickly see where they stand, and many are familiar with this type of evaluation from former school days. However, although this form of data collection and reporting might appear objective, checklists often fail to capture the complexities associated with teaching and learning. Rich descriptions of a person's performance, together with evidence to support these descriptions, provide a more comprehensive portrayal of strengths as well as areas needing improvement. While checklists are expedient, and have their place in gathering unambiguous data, we suggest that more detailed descriptions of a person's effectiveness increase an evaluation's authenticity and usefulness.

Rubrics

Rubrics, charts describing levels of proficiency, provide clear indications of a person's effectiveness at various levels of competency. Providing explicit descriptors helps all participants clarify the expectations for a particular task, and what might be done to achieve those expectations.

The rubric in this section (see Figure 11.1) was written with the assistance of several cooperating teachers and describes four levels of proficiency. It is provided as a beginning framework and readers should feel free to change, modify, or omit certain categories to suit their particular situations. Cooperating teachers and faculty advisors can then share the weekly observations, together with levels of proficiency, with their student teachers. As well, student teachers can develop and use rubrics on a weekly basis to evaluate their own levels of effectiveness. Discussions of these formative evaluations, together with considerations of what the student teacher can work towards in the following week, provide a plan for future growth as well as evidence for the summative report.

Student teachers usually appreciate the guidance associated with the mentoring process of formative evaluation, and cooperating teachers generally find this component more rewarding and less stressful than the summative evaluation involved in writing the final report. In the next section we will discuss the cooperating teacher's other responsibility, that of gatekeeper and writer of the summative report.

FIGURE 11.1:   A Rubric to Assist Formative Evaluation

Key Traits/Elements	Level 1	Level 2	Level 3	Level 4
Academic/Content Background and Knowledge	Demonstrates little knowledge of the content and how to transform it so as to make the learning accessible	Demonstrates partial knowledge of the content and how to transform it so as to make the learning accessible	Demonstrates substantial knowledge of the content and how to transform it so as to make the learning accessible	Demonstrates a thorough knowledge of the content and how to transform it so as to make the learning accessible
Organization and Preparation a) Prepared to teach	Rarely prepared and organized to teach an effective lesson	Sometimes prepared and organized to teach an effective lesson	Usually well-prepared and organized to teach an effective lesson	Consistently well-prepared and organized to teach an effective lesson
b) Accounts for individual differences	Rarely considers individual needs	With assistance sometimes modifies lessons to meet individual needs and abilities	With minimal assistance frequently modifies and adapts lessons to meet individual needs and abilities	Appropriately modifies and adapts lessons to meet the students' individual needs and abilities
Communication with Students a) Uses a variety of appropriate teaching and assessment strategies	Rarely uses effective teaching and assessment strategies	With moderate assistance employs appropriate teaching and learning strategies	Often uses a variety of appropriate teaching and assessment strategies	Consistently uses a variety of appropriate teaching and assessment strategies
b) Positive, supportive, sincere, and professional	Interactions with students are inappropriate. Rarely positive or supportive	Sometimes positive and supportive. Occasionally interacts professionally and appropriately	Usually professional, sincere, supportive and positive when interacting with students	Consistently positive, supportive, sincere and professional when interacting with students
Classroom Management a) Maintains control and on-task behaviour	Rarely uses effective strategies in dealing with inappropriate behaviours	Sometimes reacts to learners' inappropriate behaviours effectively and is beginning to establish a positive atmosphere	Often reacts to learners' inappropriate behaviours effectively and attempts to use proactive strategies to set an effective tone	Consistently uses proactive strategies in responding to learners' behaviours, and establishes a positive environment to encourage mutual respect
b) Maintains/establishes appropriate routines	Rarely follows established routines	Incorporates cooperating teacher's established routines	Implements new routines as the situation requires	Implements a clear, rational process for new routines
Other Professional Qualities a) Able to reflect and evaluate own growth	Not aware of strengths and unable to identify areas that require improvement	With assistance is able to identify strengths and areas which need to be improved	Frequently identifies areas of strength as well as areas for future growth	Consistently reflects accurately on aspects associated with professional growth and development
b) Team player	Does not work well on a team	Has difficulty working on a team	Is a team player	A team builder
c) Appearance, attitude, and demeanour	Appearance, attitude and demeanour are not those of a professional teacher	Sometimes demonstrates the attributes of a professional teacher	Frequently demonstrates the attributes of a professional teacher	Consistently demonstrates the appearance, attitude and demeanour of a professional teacher

COOPERATING TEACHERS' RESPONSIBILITY TO THE PROFESSION: THE ROLE OF GATEKEEPER

Few student teachers fail their practicum; similarly, few teachers are dismissed for incompetence. Yet, when we discuss evaluation with cooperating teachers and faculty, horror stories of a few inept student teachers surface quickly. In fact, many cooperating teachers withdraw from their supervisory role after a negative experience because it is so stressful. Obviously, policies have to be in place to deal with the task of preventing even a small number of unsuitable people from entering the profession, and in this section we explore the supervisor's responsibility of functioning as a gatekeeper.

Perhaps, because there is no common understanding of what constitutes good teaching, cooperating teachers and faculty advisors often find themselves trying to measure what seems to be unmeasurable, and trying to predict the unpredictable. The Ontario Royal Commission on Learning (1994) cautiously lists five characteristics of good teaching:

- teachers care about and are committed to students and their learning

- teachers know the subjects they teach and how to teach the material to students

- guided by clear goals, teachers manage and monitor students' learning

- teachers learn from and collaborate with others, including students, colleagues, parents, and the community

- teachers critically examine their own practice and continue to learn throughout their careers

(Ontario Ministry of Education and Training, 1994, pp. 77–78).

When writing the summative report, it can be helpful to use the list above as a guide for determining whether or not a student teacher has the aptitude to become a competent teacher.

It is through the final report that cooperating teachers convey their decision about a student teacher's potential as a practicing professional. It should be a clear summary of the growth and abilities (or lack of them) that the student teacher has demonstrated. If formative evaluation has occurred and has progressed as it should, then the summative report provides an overview of the major considerations discussed by the cooperating teacher and student teacher during the practicum experience. By the time the summative report is written, the student teacher should be fully aware of its contents (Orlich et al, 1994). The format of summative practice teaching reports varies in style from the writing of anecdotal comments to the completion of lengthy checklists. Final marks are most often reported through the use of letter grades or a pass/fail system and the method used by the institution is often based on the philosophical framework of a particular faculty in consultation with teachers in schools.

Many would argue that the practicum report is the most reliable predictor of a student teacher's future success; school districts certainly rely a great deal on them when hiring new teachers. Consequently, how these reports are composed plays an important role in determining if a new teacher will be hired. Such responsibility might well seem in stark contrast with the other role (discussed earlier) that cooperating teachers are expected to fulfill—that of guide or mentor.

MANAGING THE DILEMMA OR RESOLVING THE PROBLEM?

Andrews and Barnes (1990) contend that the two roles of formative and summative evaluation are contradictory and that it is impossible for cooperating teachers to perform both tasks simultaneously (p. 570). They write of their concern for the fairness and accuracy of the judgements made on such evaluations. If one accepts this perspective, the roles of mentor and gatekeeper would need to be assigned to different individuals. We would suggest, however, that separating the two roles would create a more serious predicament than the one with which we are presently confronted. Whatever evaluation strategies faculty advisors and cooperating teachers employ, it is important to ensure that

- the evaluation clearly indicates what the student teacher has accomplished as well as aspects that still need improvement

- whenever possible, context and evidence are included to clarify a particular comment

- formative evaluation data have been used to complete the summative evaluation form

- the student teacher has an opportunity to read and ask for clarification of any concerns expressed by the teacher educator

- the complex integration of skills, knowledge, values, attitudes, and dispositions are reflected as meaningfully as possible

Consequently, we argue that defensible formative and summative reports are best written by evaluators who have been in contact with student teachers over extended time frames, most likely cooperating teachers, because they are in ideal settings to regularly and systematically collect data from which to construct the summative report. Also, if context and evidence are meaningful criteria to be included when completing the summative reports, then cooperating teachers are generally in the best positions to provide it.

Treating the situation as a dilemma to be managed provides an opportunity to focus on the positive aspects associated with conflicting positions and to deal with the limitations of the situation. Surfacing the tensions and discussing teaching as a continuum along which everyone travels provides an environment for growth. Most student teachers appreciate constructive feedback and are only disconcerted when they do not receive opportunities to overcome significant weaknesses prior to the final report. Assuring student teachers that their strengths will be highlighted, and that only when a serious weakness shows little evidence of amelioration will it be reported on the summative report, reduces the student teacher's anxiety, and allows the contradictory roles of mentor and gatekeeper to be managed, if not resolved. Focusing on growth needs to be the prime consideration for cooperating teachers when evaluating and assisting student teachers in learning their craft. Teaching can then be regarded as a developmental journey that everyone travels, some faster than others, but not so quickly that one fails to recognize one's strengths as well as one's weaknesses. It is only when novice teachers acquire that knowledge, and develop a sense of confidence pertaining to the task before them, that they can mature to their full potential.

Painting a Picture of Reality: An Investigation of the Value of Helen's Reports

As Helen approached the end of her post-baccalaureate one-year teacher education program in secondary language teaching and social studies, and was about to begin her final practicum, she found herself reflecting on the program. The year had been stimulating, mentally and physically, and a lot more challenging than she had expected. Prior to her entry into teacher education, Helen had spent four years completing an honours undergraduate degree and graduated on the Dean's Honour Roll. This commitment to her university program, coupled with a part-time clerical job, left Helen little time to volunteer and gain experience in the local schools. She remembered feeling inadequate and unprepared as she began her pre-service program. Nevertheless, she relished the challenge and, over the course of the year, felt that she had "survived" the challenge and exceeded her own expectations. Helen discovered that she was truly committed to teaching and was certain that she would become a good teacher.

Helen had enjoyed her first three student teaching sessions. She liked the pupils, admired the teachers she met, and was challenged by the entire experience. Yet, when she reflected on her teaching, and recalled the reports her cooperating teachers had written, she was not satisfied. Something was missing. Although all of her reports consistently commented on her abilities as a teacher, she felt that they did not reflect a true picture of her

professional capabilities. The reports were complimentary but seldom mentioned what she needed to do to become a better teacher. Helen found the language vague, ambiguous, and sometimes simply "technocratic gobbledy-gook." In spite of this, Helen never raised her concerns with her cooperating teachers or faculty advisor. She signed the reports dutifully. They were positive, and she assumed that they would likely get her a job interview.

During her last practicum she had a cooperating teacher, Manuel, whom she admired greatly as a teacher and colleague. Helen felt that this might be a good opportunity to air her concerns about the reports she had received thus far (see Figure 11.2). She hoped that together they could reach a solution that would make the last report somehow "better." She showed her three reports to Manuel, and together they discussed the complexity of report writing. Manuel read her reports with some interest and seemed to agree with her concerns. Helen left their meeting believing that Manuel's report would be different.

Manuel left their meeting feeling that he understood Helen's concerns. However, the task of writing a final report was not simply a matter of addressing the student teacher's concerns. He also had a responsibility to provide a clear evaluation of Helen's strengths and weaknesses for the guidance of potential employers. As he saw it, he faced a dilemma! How could he write an accurate report that would be helpful to Helen's continued professional development, yet not endanger her chances of getting an interview at a time when teaching positions were scarce. The report had to contain specific, helpful suggestions for Helen while being diplomatic, positive, and preferably free of educational jargon. How does one write such a report? Manuel agonized about this for several days, and then wrote a report he considered fair and constructive. Helen read Manuel's report with some chagrin and felt that, even though this one was somewhat better than the others were, it still did not paint an accurate picture of her abilities as a teacher. Noting her displeasure, Manuel asked if she could suggest any changes. Feeling uncomfortable, Helen declined.

FIGURE 11.2:   Helen's Reports

The reports were originally handwritten and have been typed for ease of reading, anonymity, and consistency. Except for the pseudonym Helen, we have not edited the reports in any way, or corrected any of the spelling or grammatical errors.

Report A

Student: Helen   Program: Social Science

Unit taught

Objectives:
   The 1920's "Emancipation of Women" unit
   audio strip - introduction
   hand-out-problem study for group work

Presentation:
   resources well used
   Helen is thorough, well organized and moves lesson nicely
   interesting problem study

Questioning Ability:
   excellent questioning techniques
   students were very interested and responded well
   good use of blackboard

Personal Qualities:
   Very valuable interesting unit. Helen is a good leader, very interested in the lesson content herself, pleasant and business like. She is doing excellent work and will make a fine teacher.

Basic Strengths/Constructive Suggestions for Improvement:
   Helen is progressing well.

FIGURE 11.2:   Helen's Reports (cont'd)

Report B

Student: Helen   Program: French

6 lesson taught; attended board P.D. day

Academic Background:
  Very good grasp of subject matter. Helen showed initiative in the use of resources. Lessons and student assignments were suitable planned.

Objectives:
  Curriculum objectives were adequately met.

Presentation:
  A good level of interest and participation was maintained in most lessons. Directions were clear, class control good and a variety of teaching approaches were used appropriate to an advanced class.

Questioning Ability:
  Good questioning techniques were used. Helen is quick to build on students' answers and allow scope for discussion.

Personal Qualities:
  Listens to student answers, remains calm and in control.

Basic Strengths/Constructive Suggestions for Improvement:
  Good questioning techniques - encourages discussion - aroused student interest in the story in social sc. - willing to use a variety of techniques - use students' names during lesson - outline evaluation criteria for group work before students proceed to their groups.

Helen's teaching situation was clearly satisfactory.

Report C

Student: Helen   Program: French

13 grade 10 classes 6 grade 11 classes and 2 OAC classes as well as library duty, study hall supervision and attended our PD Day activities. She prepared several tests and work sheets.

Academic Background:
  Helen has a very strong French background - she is very keen on passing her interest in French to her students. Her materials are suitable for the students and she prepares well.

Objectives:
  Her objectives are clear and are appropriate as described above. Helen can make accurate statements about the accomplishment or non-accomplishment of objectives after the class is completed.

FIGURE 11.2: Helen's Reports (cont'd)

Presentation:
Helen is usually able to maintain an interest level, which appears "normal" for the particular group and topic. Pupil participation is at a good level in a majority of lessons. She maintains control for effective learning.

Questioning Ability:
She practices effective questioning techniques.

Personal Qualities:
Helen always appears in complete control of self and situation and has a consistent calm, firm, professional classroom manner. she accepts advice and criticism in a constructive way.

Basic Strengths/Constructive Suggestions for Improvement:
is always in control - has a wide knowledge of contemporary French - shows real interest in the students and their progress - be sure to adapt the class in action when things seem to "stall" a bit - watch pace with general level.

It was a pleasure having Helen. She will make a fine teacher.

Manuel's Report

Student: Helen   Program: Social Science

Helen taught several lessons to an advanced grade 11 class and 4 different lessons to an OAC class.

Academic Background:
excellent knowledge of subject matter taught
most lessons were very well organized with clear direction, focus
materials selected for student study were very appropriate to the level of the class

Objectives:
most objectives in the cognitive domain, try to keep a clear objective for each part of the lesson and try to use some affective objectives as well

Presentation:
excellent variety of methodology displayed in group work, debate, use of filmstrips, transparencies, document study, what if situations

Questioning Ability:
evidence of logical sequencing, good clarity of questions, a number of evaluative questions also, ability to rearrange questions to develop a particular concept that created some difficulty for the students

Personal Qualities:
excellent enthusiasm and interest in subject matter and students, good ability to self-evaluate was requiring refinement

Basic Strengths/Constructive Suggestions for Improvement:
creative use of various teaching tech. and willingness to use a variety of methodology - board work easy to read - excellent knowledge and interest, good rapport - work on variety of response to student answers - continue to involve students who do not raise hands - try to develop student board outlines, titles. Helen is performing very well and will be an excellent asset to a school's teaching staff. Her abilities, flexibility, and enthusiasm are admirable.

QUESTIONS

Framing, Reframing, and Exploring Solutions

1. Figure 11.2 contains Helen's reports. Read each report and write a brief description of Helen's strengths, weaknesses, and ways for her to improve, based on the information given in each of the reports. What are the similarities in each report? How does each report differ? In what ways do the reports paint a clear picture of Helen's strengths, weaknesses, and potential as a teacher?

2. What were the tensions between Helen and Manuel? How can they be surfaced? Should they be surfaced? If so, at which stages of a student teacher's development should tension be surfaced? How might the Johari Window (see Chapter 7) be used to assist the communication process between Helen and Manuel?

3. Considering Helen's concerns, are they that the reports did not accurately describe her abilities or that they did not mention what she needed to accomplish to become a better teacher? What do you think Helen was looking for in a "better" report? Frame, then reframe these questions from
   a) Helen's perspective
   b) the cooperating teacher's perspective
   c) the faculty advisor's perspective

4. How might the cooperating teachers and Helen have used some of the evaluation strategies discussed in this chapter (e.g., journals, self-evaluation, and peer evaluation) to improve the reports and help Helen understand their value?

5. What are some effective strategies for using a rubric so that
   a) student teachers are aware of the qualities the cooperating teacher considers a strength, as well as recognizing elements that require increased consideration?
   b) cooperating teachers are aware of how student teachers are evaluating themselves?

Personal Reflections and Connections

1. Have you experienced a situation similar to the one in the case study? If so, what was your reaction at the time? What do you think would be your reaction to a similar situation today? What are the reasons for any changes in your perspective of the situation?

2. This case illustrates that there are often three reasons for writing summative reports for student teachers at the end of the practicum. One reason is to inform the student teachers about their progress as developing professionals; the second is to submit an evaluation to the university; the third is to serve as a reference for employment in teaching. These purposes may seem contradictory in nature. Can cooperating teachers accomplish all three on one form?
   a) If you believe that cooperating teachers' reports can accomplish all purposes, how can it be done?
   b) If you believe that it cannot be done, what solution(s) do you suggest?

3. As a student teacher, think about the feedback that you need. Do you want comments that will assist you in becoming a better teacher or are you looking for a report that will help you secure employment?

a) Is it possible to receive both? How?

b) What are your responsibilities in this endeavour?

4. As a cooperating teacher, reflect on how you use data collected during formative evaluation to write your student teacher's summative report. Are there other strategies that might be valuable? If so, what are they, and why?

5. Discuss the methods from this chapter that you consider most useful. What are the reasons for your choices?

Reflections on Learning-to-Teach

1. Is it possible for cooperating teachers to act as mentors and, at the same time, serve as gatekeepers for the profession?

a) If so, discuss approaches for accomplishing both tasks, while addressing the obstacles that have to be overcome.

b) If not, discuss changes that might be made to the practicum model to improve supervision and evaluation.

ENDNOTE

1. Throughout this chapter we use the term *evaluation* to include both the collecting and recording of evidence of a student teacher's growth and development (frequently called assessment), and making a judgement, or placing a value, on that growth and development based on the evidence.

TOWARDS A TEACHER VOICE IN EDUCATIONAL REFORM: PREPARING NOVICE TEACHERS TO BECOME AGENTS OF CHANGE

Today an ever increasing number of voices call for educational reform—business groups, parent groups, and political parties, even agricultural associations, environmental groups, and seniors groups. In our increasingly pluralistic, democratic society this is to be expected. Schools, no less than the media, provide a potent vehicle for a plethora of groups to present their viewpoints to the young. As a result, fierce debate has erupted about how to shape both the curriculum and the character of schooling. What is surprising, however, is the virtual absence of strong, articulate teachers' voices. Surely, the views of the professionals charged with the task of teaching our children need to be voiced in the debate about educational reform. No doubt a variety of reasons exist for this. Of central importance, however, would appear to be adoption of a view of the legitimate role of teachers as following the prescriptions of more responsible authority. Until relatively recently, teachers have been seen (and saw themselves) more as functionaries than professionals delivering the prescribed curriculum, and generally conforming to the prescriptions of school boards and education ministries.

Unfortunately the one-size-fits-all nature of many reforms has produced ambiguous results and left behind a disillusioned public. Frequently, teachers are blamed for the excesses of reforms such as the new math, whole language, values clarification, the use of calculators, or child-centred education. What has become apparent is that teachers need to become an integral part of educational reform, because action is far more potent than reaction, and more importantly, because their input is critical for success.

TEACHERS AS AGENTS OF CHANGE—THE CENTRALITY OF TEACHER PREPARATION

As discussed in Chapter 1, not only is much teacher knowledge tacit in nature, but teachers lack a language with which to effectively articulate their knowledge. This means that if teachers are to contribute to educational reform, they need to surface and articulate what they know about learners, subject matter, and the complex process of facilitating learning. More than this, they need to share, challenge, and explore the utility of their knowledge in a systematic manner that not only explicates teacher knowledge, but also increases public confidence. We have referred to this kind of activity as a *scholarship of pedagogy*. By joining professional communities of inquiry to study teaching and learning, teachers take the first steps essential to raising authoritative voices in the ongoing debate.

In this book, we have laid a foundation for establishing such communities among cooperating teachers, faculty advisors, and student teachers in the service of learning-to-teach. By providing sets of concepts for making sense of teaching and learning-to-teach, and then engaging readers in a process of exploring their utility, we have attempted to give critical inquiry a central place in learning-to-teach. In doing so, we have intentionally opened up the processes and structures of teacher preparation for critical examination by novice teachers. Some might suggest that novice teachers because of their inexperience and vulnerability should not engage in such critique. (Certainly, the cases included in previous chapters have highlighted both the daunting nature of learning-to-teach, and the vulnerability of student teachers.) However, the very complex, indeterminate, and conflicting nature of teaching and learning-to-teach suggests to us that very early on, novice teachers need to assume a critical stance on the *what is* in teacher education, in light of the visions they construct of *what could be*. If later on in their careers teachers are to have voices in broad educational reform, then during teacher preparation, novice teachers need to learn to take on the role of *agents of change*.

In order to examine how we construct and organize what students experience in their education, the case studies in this book have focussed on some of the central issues in learning-to-teach: communication, relationships, practice, analytic reflection, dilemma management, social justice, inclusion. Through a variety of cases involving student teachers, cooperating teachers, and faculty advisors, we have constructed a picture of teacher preparation as it currently exists. Hopefully in engaging these cases, our readers have entered a critical dialogue with other students and teacher educators about teaching and learning-to-teach. While it is important to describe *what is* in teacher education, it is perhaps more important and relevant to suggest *what could be*. In this final chapter, we attempt to explore what teacher education could be like by examining the current situation, and we also look at what it would take to create teachers who would develop the voice needed to create systematic and logical educational reform. We begin by revisiting some of the issues raised earlier, both to outline the challenges and to articulate fruitful possibilities. We then present the views of a respected school principal on the possibilities and problems of viewing novice teachers as agents of change—views that are much more positive than we might have expected from someone immersed in the realities of public schooling. We conclude with a brief survey of what we see as promising sites for cooperating teachers, faculty advisors, and student teachers to explore the possibilities in learning-to-teach in order to allow novices to have the needed voice.

CHALLENGING THE *WHAT IS* AND CONSIDERING THE *WHAT COULD BE* OF TEACHER PREPARATION—THREE PERSPECTIVES

In exploring the present reality of teacher preparation, we explore and review the situations of each of three members of the practicum triad—the student teachers, the cooperating teacher, and the faculty advisor.

The *What Is* and *What Could Be* for Student Teachers

Typically, student teachers enter teacher preparation programs with restricted ways of thinking about teaching, learning, subject matter, and schooling. Because of their experiences as successful pupils and their very potent images of competent teachers and good pupils, they are predisposed to support schooling as it is (McIntyre & Byrd, 1996). Most student teachers have never questioned the efficacy of schooling or the role of teachers in it. Rather, they envisage themselves as assuming the role of teacher as they experienced it. Unfortunately, as they all too quickly learn, their experiences as pupils are not representative of those of the majority of pupils they will teach. Nor will the schooling they had prepare their pupils for today's rapidly changing world. Unless preservice teachers' views are challenged during teacher preparation, particularly during student teaching, they will be the least likely to promote, or even think about, change in the educational system.

As the case studies in this book illustrate, student teachers continually confront dilemmas, contradictions, tensions, and anxieties with which they are ill-prepared to deal. Characteristically, they underestimate the demands and the complexity of learning-to-teach, expecting their movement from student to teacher to be smooth. They are surprised, troubled, and even angry when they find that their preconceptions are incorrect.

Faced with the unexpected complexity and tensions of learning-to-teach, student teachers cannot help but be impressed by the expertise their cooperating teachers demonstrate daily. They talk frequently about their respect for the cooperating teachers with whom they work, and typically tend to fit into things as they are. If they are successful in fitting in, this congruence with their mentor provides a real sense of *being a teacher*. It also gives them a sense of comfort and control, even though they have had little to do with setting up the classroom routines and pupil expectations that make the smooth running of the class possible. On the other hand, this ready identification with their cooperating teachers can place student teachers in conflict with their university course work. Typically, they see university professors as somewhat isolated from the reality of classrooms, and as raising issues far removed from student teachers' immediate concerns with getting through lessons and keeping rambunctious pupils on task. It may only be several years into their careers that novice teachers come to understand and appreciate their professors' concerns with issues such as equity, inclusion, and cognitive development. In the meantime, as they wrestle with the immediate concerns of learning-to-teach, they have difficulty seeing the relevance of theory. Learning-to-teach needs to be a time "when desires are rehearsed, refashioned, and refused," and student teachers are involved in the construction of the "real, the necessary, and the imaginary" (Britzman, 1991, p. 220). Without the critical interrogation of *what is* in schools that university course work should promote, the *what could be* is all too easily overlooked.

In learning-to teach, student teachers are caught between two contested worlds. On the one hand, they struggle to construct active identities as classroom teachers; on the other, in university classrooms they slide back into the relatively passive role of student. This "fragmented experience" (Britzman, 1991) contributes significantly to the strains and confusion student teachers experience as they struggle to construct their own teaching identities in borrowed classrooms. Ideally, their identities will evolve in a process of continual change, becoming increasingly complex with more experience and time to reflect on it with more experienced colleagues. And while the split between the worlds of the university and the schools complicates the task of developing a coherent identity, it also has the potential to prompt critical examination of both.

This outline of the student teacher experience in learning-to-teach makes it clear that novice teachers are likely to emerge from teacher preparation with some confusion about their identities as teachers. The task of developing in student teachers the skills, dispositions, and motivation to begin to take on a role of change agent will not be an easy one.

The *What Is* and *What Could Be* for Cooperating Teachers

Without question, cooperating teachers significantly influence the professional development of student teachers. Their beliefs and practices have an overwhelming influence on the beliefs and practices student teachers acquire. Both student teachers and cooperating teachers perceive cooperating teachers as making the most significant and relevant contribution to student teachers' development.

Cooperating teachers volunteer or are selected by school administrators and typically receive no training for their additional responsibilities as a teacher educator. Little financial incentive and no workload accommodation are provided for taking on this role. Cooperating teachers assume teacher education responsibilities in addition to their full-time teaching and other responsibilities. While they take on the role for a variety of reasons, typically these have something to do with their sense of responsibility to the profession. Some see acting as a cooperating teacher as an opportunity to repay the system for their own teacher education, or to share or pass on the beliefs and practices they have acquired. Others look on it as an opportunity for professional growth—through hearing about new teaching techniques or having opportunities to explore and question their own practices from a different perspective. Others find the experience gratifying, especially when their student teachers observe and practise their own strategies with their pupils.

Typically, cooperating teachers see themselves as mentors with little or no power over student teachers. Until they encounter a truly problematic student, they are unlikely to be aware of their role as gatekeeper to the profession. They see the world of learning-to-teach through the immediacy of daily mentoring experiences with student teachers in their classrooms, and give little thought to the future of the profession or the educational system.

Student teachers are quite conscious of their cooperating teachers' power. They know the importance of teaching reports in securing their first teaching positions, and are quite attuned to what their cooperating teachers might want. They enjoy the personal, one-on-one attention of cooperating teachers who observe and comment insightfully on their practice and growth. Such individualized attention creates a powerful learning experience that meshes with their strong desire to engage in ongoing, personalized discussion. Similarly, cooperating teachers often appreciate the opportunity to talk at length about the problems and success of their teaching with another adult, who also brings current ideas from the university. It really is not surprising then that student teachers so readily accept and adopt their cooperating teachers' beliefs and practices. Student teachers are working with dynamic, experienced teachers, recognized (however marginally) for their expertise and competence. Consequently, the cooperating teachers' actions and discourse constitute a very powerful instructional tool. The personal, intense environment of the school setting encourages student teachers to adopt current school practices—sometimes without the critical scrutiny that they deserve— simply because they are perceived "to work." Such a process of enculturation does little to promote either student or cooperating teachers as agents of change, or the engagement in the *scholarship of pedagogy* needed to equip teachers with a legitimate voice in reform.

The *What Is* and *What Could Be* for University-Based Teacher Educators

University-based teacher educators, through the faculty courses they deliver, also play a significant role. At the same time, they cannot help but be aware that student teachers question the relevance of what they hear, and that they are impatient to get on with "real learning-to-teach" in the practicum. Typically they struggle with the dilemma of how to address student teachers' immediate concerns without sacrificing the broader critique needed for continued professional growth and for becoming agents of change. At the same time, professors enjoy the status associated with being at a university. Student teachers may well admire professors' knowledge and research, and struggle to discern its immediate relevance. However, the reality of practicum experience can produce a distinct narrowing of concern in novice teachers   particularly when cooperating teachers themselves limit their concern to the *what is* of the classroom and lose sight of *what could be*. If novice teachers are to be prepared to become agents of change, it seems apparent that ways must be found for cooperating teachers and university faculty to construct more productive collaborations.

As explored in Chapter 6, the responsibilities of education professors are not limited to the instruction of preservice students. Their roles, like their school-based colleagues', are both complex and fragmented. They teach preservice and graduate students, conduct research, write, and publish. They frequently serve on school, ministry, faculty, and community committees charged with a variety of responsibilities, while at the same time filling demanding administrative roles. Their roles as teacher educators and university researchers do not mesh easily. The relative independence of individual professors tends to mitigate against development of a coherent perspective on learning-to-teach across a teacher preparation program. And while the ferment of conflicting ideas may be intellectually stimulating, it works against the delivery of a coherent program. As teacher educators, university professors may be drawn to a variety of professional activities—including extensive involvement in the practicum. However, they quickly learn that the university merit system values research productivity more highly than professional responsibilities. New professors, with probationary appointments for five or more years, are under considerable pressure to develop the substantial research records required for permanent tenured status.

The structure and accepted practices of university teaching also contribute to the fragmentation of education professors' experiences. Professors who may be involved with research on more innovative instructional practices typically find themselves restrained by conservative university perspectives on instruction. This results in anomalies such as lectures for 100 or more student teachers on individual differences or active learning; courses on diverse assessment strategies evaluated by multiple choice examinations; lectures on inclusion delivered in auditoriums that make little provision for the hearing impaired. It is hard not to see these anomalies actively working against professors' explicit instruction. More significantly, they undermine any intentions to prepare novice teachers for the role of change agents in schools.

YOUNG TEACHERS AS AGENTS OF CHANGE—A VIEW FROM THE PRINCIPAL'S DESK

There is little question that our examination of the *what is* and our exploration of the *what could be* of learning-to-teach has revealed the variety of factors that conspire against creating teachers who can take on active roles as agents of change in the schools, the universities, and in society. Nevertheless, engaging novice teachers in a critical examination of their own learning-to-teach would appear to hold some potential in this regard. At the same time, some educators do confront the limitations of their environments and work to change them for the better. In an attempt to provide a different perspective on the problems and possibilities of novice teachers acting as agents of change, we turned to a principal who routinely hires graduates from our teacher preparation program. What follows is his perspective on *what is* and *what could be*.

> Young teachers breathe new life and enthusiasm into our schools at a time when our current teachers feel somewhat overwhelmed by impending change, criticism from governments and the media about the shortcomings of schools, and massive cutbacks in support in the daily tasks of teaching. New teachers support our programs, bring new ideas, ask hard questions, and make unique assumptions about teaching and learning that require those of us with many years of experience to see ourselves as changing within their dynamic. New teachers become agents of change just by their very presence in our schools and most of us see that as both invigorating and inspiring.
>
> Beyond their enthusiasm though, I see most new teachers as needing to use their first few years to work through their own growth as a teacher. They are (and need to be) cautious in their teaching practices as they pay attention to developing what works for them. Sometimes, in developing their own teaching style, they tend to become one-dimensional as they try out one strategy and learn to become comfortable with that as they find ways to cover the content. They tend to worry about maintaining control of the classes, about covering the curriculum, and showing that they have standards—which are all important in their own right—but frequently they forget that there are diverse pupils in their classes, pupils with different learning styles and needs, and so on. They need the time and support to become comfortable as teachers before they can be agents of change in our schools, before they take risks. They need to ask hard questions about both the content and the methodology as they learn to focus on their students, not themselves, and they need to take leadership for their own professional learning and that within the school. The benefits to the school and to their own professional growth are obvious but the costs are present. They risk challenges and confrontation from colleagues, administrators, and parents on a daily basis if their students do not meet the "standards" expected.
>
> The current workload for new teachers in their first teaching assignment is exactly the same as that of my 33-year veteran teacher who will retire at the end of the year. There is little support built in within the system except that which we can provide within the school. Not only are new teachers required to assume the same responsibilities with the same results, but also

they are expected to assume much of the extracurricular commitments to maintain the health and well-being of the school. New teachers as change agents in the schools? I don't think we allow them that luxury (G. Beynon, 1999).

Gwyn Beynon is a secondary school principal with a firm commitment to teacher education and the role of novice teachers to school renewal. He encourages the experienced teachers on his staff to act as cooperating teachers, meets with the student teachers assigned to his school, and makes a concerted effort to hire a broad spectrum of new graduates when opportunities arise. He recognizes their need to take some time to find their identity as a teacher in the school, in the larger system, and even within themselves, and he expects them to take the time to do that. But he makes a valid point: novice teachers are at risk in their new career because of the demands placed upon them by the system and by themselves. Certainly in the beginning years of their career, novice teachers need to take care of themselves, the curriculum, and their pupils; at this point they cannot be the ones to change the existing educational system with innovative practices or beliefs. They will, however, be the ones who will be prepared to ask hard questions and to critique current practices. Their success in finding or not finding satisfactory answers may propel them to become the educational leaders who will question the status quo. They may have opportunity to develop their identity as teachers from a more transformational stance as they engage in practices and discourse, which may be seen as subversive yet productive in the long term.

These ideas can be used as a basis on which to plan for the future of teacher education policies and practices, to further explore *what could be* in teacher education. How teacher education develops depends in large part on how serious teacher educators and powerful bureaucrats become about recognizing the *what is* in the current educational system and confronting the realities. They will need to extend their vision to seeing the need to transform the educational system into one which guarantees a sound, liberal education and equal access to all, regardless of race, gender, class, sexual orientation, or physical abilities or disabilities. Student teachers need access to critical views in learning and practice so they begin to engage in discursive and active practices that will emancipate them as teachers and then, emancipate their pupils. The change required to allow novice teachers to direct change will be slow and time-consuming and cannot be merely mandated. Eisner (1992) says "one thing is clear. It is much easier to change educational policy than to change the ways in which schools function. Schools are robust institutions whose very robustness provides a source of social stability" (p. 610).

All teachers, whether administrators or classroom teachers, university professors, or student teachers, must recognize their role as teacher educators in a community of professional practice. In this book, we have advocated that this community must develop an articulation of a scholarship of pedagogy that is conducted publicly, is subject to the critical review of the community, and is used, modified, and built upon by those professional colleagues. This is needed to promote a transformative process of teacher education that will always remain complex but accessible for both teacher learners and teacher educators. We have presented varied concepts, issues, case studies, and activities that we believe will promote the kind of open and transformative practices to enable an improved, community-based process of teacher education for novice teachers and teacher educators. At the same time, the process should support each member of the community in the articulation and development of their practice. We are aware that our views are risky and largely untried in current times, and we welcome collegial review and comment from all members of the community. We hope that this book will promote active discussion and further research into the professional practice of educating teachers.

QUESTIONS

Personal Reflections and Connections:

1. What kind of teacher are you? What kind of teacher do you *want* to be? What kind of teacher are you *allowed* to be? Is there a difference? Explain.

Pondering the Future

1. Consider your own preferences for learning-to-teach. Describe the *what could be*—the ideal teacher education program for someone like you to become the best possible teacher.

2. How would your ideal program vary from traditional forms of teacher education? What would be the benefits of your proposed model and the weaknesses?

3. Could such a program be implemented? Why or why not?

4. Would such a model have an impact on or change the educational system in the twenty-first century in any way? How?

REFERENCES

Acheson, K., & Gall, M. (1992). *Techniques in the clinical supervision of teachers* (3rd ed.). New York: Longman.

Ackoff, R. (1979). The future of operational research is past. *Journal of Operational Research Society, 30*(2), 93–104.

Adkins, C. (1999). Toward an equal playing field: The role of the university faculty from a mentor teacher perspective. In P. Graham, S. Hudson-Ross, C. Adkins, P. McWhorter, & J. McDuffie-Stewart, *Teacher mentor: A dialogue for collaborative learning* (pp. 157–162). New York: Teachers College Press.

Andrews, J. (Ed.). (1996). *Teaching students with diverse needs: Elementary classrooms.* Toronto: Nelson Canada.

Andrews, T.E., & Barnes, S. (1990). Assessment of teaching. In W.R. Houston (Ed.), *Handbook of research on teacher education* (pp. 569–598). New York: MacMillan Inc.

Apple, M. (1982). *Education and power.* Boston: Routledge.

Bandura, A. (Ed.). (1995). *Self-efficacy in changing societies.* New York: Cambridge University Press.

Bandy, H., & Alexander, S. (1988). A team approach to student teacher supervision. In P. Holborn, M. Wideen & I. Andrews (Eds.), *Becoming a teacher* (pp. 263–270). Toronto: Kagan & Woo.

Barnes, D. (1992). The significance of teachers' frames for teaching. In T. Russell and H. Munby (Eds.), *Teachers and teaching: From classroom to reflection* (pp. 9–32). London: Falmer.

Barnes, S., & Edwards, S. (1984). *Effective student teaching experiences: A qualitative-quantitative study.* Austin, TX: Research and Development Center for Teacher Education.

Ben-Peretz, M., & Rumney, S. (1991). Professional thinking in guided practice. *Teaching and Teacher Education, 7*(5/6), 517–530.

Berard, R. N. (1988). The evaluation of student teaching. In P. Holborn, M. Wideen, & I. Andrews (Eds.), *Becoming a teacher* (pp. 210–222). Toronto: Kagan & Woo.

Berliner, D. (1988). Some views of effective teaching and a simple theory of classroom instruction. In D. Berliner & B. Rosenshine (Eds.), *Talks to teachers* (pp. 93–110). New York: Random House.

Berliner, D. C. (1990). If the metaphor fits, why not wear it? The teacher as executive. *Theory into Practice, 29*(2), 85–93.

Beynon, C. A. (1994). I thought I knew how to teach: A beginning music teacher's reflections about learning to teach. *Canadian Music Educator, 35*(6), 17–26.

Beynon, C. A. (1997). Crossing over from student to teacher: Negotiating an identity. Unpublished doctoral dissertation. Toronto: The University of Toronto.

Blackmore, J., & Kenway, J. (1995). Changing schools, teachers and curriculum: But what about the girls? In D. Corson (Ed.), *Discourse and power in educational organizations* (pp. 233–256). Toronto: OISE Press.

Bourdieu, P. (1977). *Outline of theory and practice.* London: Cambridge.

Britzman, D. P. (1991). *Practice makes practice: A critical study of learning to teach*. New York: State University of New York Press.

Brown, M. & Fasano, J. (1996). Instructional strategies for meeting the learning needs of all students in the classroom. In J. Andrews (Ed.), *Teaching students with diverse needs: Secondary classrooms*. Toronto: Nelson Canada.

Bullough, R.V. (1994). Digging at the roots: Discipline, management, and metaphor. *Action in Teacher Education, 16*, 1–10.

Calderhead, J. (1987). The quality of reflection in student teachers' professional learning. *European Journal of Teacher Education, 10*(3), 269–278.

Carnegie Forum on Education and the Economy. (1986). *A nation prepared: Teaching for the 21st century*. New York: Carnegie Forum on Education and the Economy.

Chi, M. T. H., Feltovich, P. J., & Glaser, R. (1981). Categorization and representation of physics problems by experts and novices. *Cognitive Science, 5*, 121–152.

Clark, C. M. (1988). Asking the right questions about teacher preparation: Contributions of research on teaching. *Educational Researcher, 17*(2), 5–12.

Cochran-Smith, M. (1991). Reinventing student teaching. *Journal of Teacher Education, 42*, 104–118.

Cohen, L. G. & Spenciner, L. J. (1998). *Assessment of children and youth*. New York: Addison Wesley, Longman Inc.

Corson, D. (1993). *Language, minority education and gender: Linking social justice and power*. Toronto: OISE Press.

Crealock, C., & Laine, C. J. (1996). The exceptional student: Rethinking current practice. In G. Milburn (Ed.), *Ring some alarm bells: Reactions to the report of the royal commission on learning*. (pp. 109–118). London, ON: Althouse Press.

Cuban, L. (1992). Managing dilemmas while building educational communities. *Educational Researcher, 21*(1), 4–11.

Dewey, J. (1933). *How we think: A restatement of the relation of reflective thinking to the educative process*. Lexington, MA: D. C. Heath.

Doyle, W. (1986). Classroom organization and management. In M. C. Wittrock (Ed.), *A Handbook of research on teaching*. New York: MacMillan.

Doyle, W. (1990). Themes in teacher education research. In W. R. Houston (Ed.), *Handbook of educational research on teacher education* (pp.3–24). New York: MacMillan.

Eisener, E. (1992). Educational reform and the ecology of schooling. *Teachers College Record, 93*, 610–627

Fasano, J., & Brown, M. (1992). Facilitating inclusive secondary classrooms through curriculum adaption. *Exceptionality Education Canada, 2*(1&2), 155–179.

Feiman-Nemser, S., & Buchmann, M. (1987). When is student teaching teacher education? *Teaching and Teacher Education, 3*(4), 255–273.

Fraser, J. W. (1992). Preparing teachers for democratic schools: The Holmes and Carnegie reports five years later–A critical reflection. *Teachers College Record, 94*, 7–55.

Freire, P. (1985). *The politics of education*. South Hadley, MA: Bergin & Garvey.

Fullan, M. (1982). *The meaning of educational change*. Toronto: OISE Press.

Gardner, H. (1991). *The unschooled mind: How children think and how schools should teach*. New York: Basic Books.

Gardner, H. (1993). *Frames of mind: The theory of multiple intelligences*. New York: Basic Books Inc.

Geddis, A. N., Lynch, M. J., & Speir, S. B. (1998). Bridging theory and practice: Towards a professional scholarship of pedagogy. *Teaching and Teacher Education, 14*(1), 96–106.

Geddis, A. N., & Roberts, D. A. (1998). As science students become science teachers: A Perspective on learning orientation. *Journal of Science Teacher Education, 9*(4), 271–292.

Giebelhaus, C. R. (1994). The mechanical third ear device: A student teaching supervision alternative. *Journal of Teacher Education, 45*(5), 365–373.

Giroux, H., & McLaren, P. (1987). Teacher education as a counterpublic sphere. In T. Popkewitz (Ed.), *Critical studies in teacher education* (pp. 298 334). London: Falmer Press.

Glickman, C. D. & Bey, T.M. (1990). Supervision. In W. R. Houston (Ed.), *Handbook of research on teacher education* (pp. 549–568). New York: MacMillan.

Gonzalez, L. E., & Carter, K. (1996). Correspondence in cooperating teachers' and student teachers' interpretations of classroom events. *Teaching and Teacher Education, 12*(1), 39–47.

Goodlad, J. I. (1990). *Teachers for our nation's schools*. San Francisco: Jossey-Bass.

Goodman, J. (1988). The political tactics and teaching strategies of reflective, active, preservice teachers. *The Elementary School Journal, 89*(1), 23–41.

Guyton, E., & McIntyre, D. J. (1990). Student teaching and school experiences. In W. R. Houston (Ed.), *Handbook of research on teacher education* (pp. 514 534). New York: MacMillan.

Harrington, H. (1991). The case as method. *Action in Teacher Education, 12*(4), 1–10

Harrington, H. L., Quinn-Leering, K., & Hodson, L. (1996). Written case analyses and critical reflection. *Teacher & Teacher Education, 12*(1), 25–37.

Hollingsworth, S. (1989). Prior beliefs and cognitive change in learning to teach. *American Educational Research Journal, 26*(2), 160–189.

Holmes Group. (1986). *Tomorrow's teachers: A report of the Holmes Group*. East Lansing, MI: Author.

Housner, L. D., & Griffey, D. C. (1986). Teacher cognition: Differences in planning and interactive decision-making between experienced and inexperienced teachers. *Research Quarterly for Exercise and Sport, 56*, 45–53.

Huling-Austin, L., Odell, S. J., Ishler, P., Kay, R. S., & Edelfelt, R. A. (1989). *Assisting the beginning teacher*. Reston, VA: Association of Teacher Educators.

Jackson, P. W. (1968). *Life in classrooms*. New York: Holt, Rinehart and Winston.

Johnston, S. (1994). Experience is the best teacher–or is it? *Journal of Teacher Education, 45*(3), 199–208.

Juliebo, M., Jackson, R., & Peterson, S. (1995). Symposium on school-university collaboration. *The Canadian Administrator, 34*(4), 1–4.

Kagan, D. (1992). Professional growth among preservice and beginning teachers. *Review of Educational Research, 62*(2), 129–169.

Katz, L. G., & Raths, J. (1992). Six dilemmas in teacher education. *Journal of Teacher Education, 43*(5), 376–385.

Knowles, G., & Cole, A. (with Presswood, N.). (1994). *Through preservice teachers' eyes: Exploring field experiences through narrative and inquiry.* Toronto: Macmillan.

Koerner, M. E. (1992). The cooperating teacher: An ambivalent participant in student teaching. *Journal of Teacher Education, 43*(1), 46–56.

Laine, C. J. (1991). Attitudes toward children by student teachers over the duration of their training. *ORBIT* (Journal of the Ontario Institute for Studies in Education), *22*(3), 22–23.

Lampert, M. (1985). How do teachers manage to teach? Perspectives on problems in practice. *Harvard Educational Review, 55*(2), 178–194.

Lasley, T. J. (1994). Teacher technicians: A "new" metaphor for new teachers. *Action in Teacher Education, 16*, 11–19.

Lavoie, R. D. (1990). *How difficult can this be?* PBS Video: Eagle Hill Foundation, Inc.

Lewis, A. (1982). *Evaluating educational personnel.* Arlington, VA: American Association of School Administrators.

Lortie, D. C. (1975). *Schoolteacher: A sociological study.* Chicago: University of Chicago Press.

MacDonald, C. J. (1993). Coping with stress during the teaching practicum: The student teacher's perspective. *The Alberta Journal of Educational Research, 39*(4), 407–418.

MacDonald, R. E., & Healy, S. D. (1999). *A handbook for beginning teachers.* (2nd ed.). New York: Longman.

Marshall, M., & Barritt, L. (1990). Choices made, worlds created: The rhetoric of AERJ. *American Educational Research Journal, 27*, 589–609.

May, S. (1994). *Making multicultural education work.* Toronto: OISE Press.

McIntyre, D. J., & Byrd, D. M. (Eds.). (1996). *Preparing tomorrow's teachers: The field experience.* Thousand oaks, CA: Corwin Press.

McLaughlin, H. J. (1994). From negation to negotiation: Moving away from the management metaphor. *Action in Teacher Education, 16*(1), 75–84.

Montgomery, K. (1997). Student teacher portfolios: A portrait of the beginning teacher. *Teacher Educator, 32*(4), 216–225.

Morine-Dershimer, G., & Tarpley Reeve, P. (1994). Prospective teachers' images of management. *Action in Teacher Education, 16*(1), 29–40.

Murray, L. B. (1993). Putting it all together at the school level: A principal's perspective. In J. I. Goodlad and T. C. Lovitt (Eds.), *Integrating general and special education.* Toronto: Maxwell Macmillan Canada.

Newell, A., & Simon, H. A. (1972). *Human problem solving.* Englewood Cliffs, NJ: Prentice-Hall.

Ontario Ministry of Education and Training (1994). *For the love of learning: Report of the Royal Commission on Learning, Volume 1.* Toronto: Queen's Printer for Ontario.

Orlich, D. C., Harder, R. J., Callahan, R. C., Kauchak, D.P., & Gibson, H. W. (1994). *Teaching strategies: A guide to better instruction (4th ed.)*. Lexington, MA: D.C. Heath and Company.

Peters, R. S. (1959). *Authority, responsibility and education*. London: George Allen & Unwin.

Peterson, K., & Kauchak, D. (1982). *Teacher evaluation: Perspectives, practices and promises*. Salt Lake City: Center for Educational Practice, University of Utah.

Popkewitz, T. (Ed.). (1987). *Critical studies in teacher education*. London: Falmer Press.

Posner, G. J. (1989). *Field experience: Methods of reflective teaching*, (2nd ed.). New York: Longman.

Rodriguez, A. J. (1993). A dose of reality: Understanding the origin of the theory/practice dichotomy in teacher education from the students' point of view. *Journal of Teacher Education, 44*(3), 213–222.

Room, A. (1985). *Dictionary of confusing words and meanings*. London: Routledge & Kegan Paul.

Scardamalia, M., & Bereiter, C. (1989). Conceptions of teaching and approaches to core problems. In M. C. Reynolds (Ed.), *Knowledge base for the beginning teacher* (pp. 37–46). New York: Pergamon.

Schön, D. A. (1983). *The reflective practitioner: How professionals think in action*. New York: Basic Books.

Schön, D. A. (1987). *Educating the reflective practitioner: Towards a new design for teaching and learning in the professions*. San Francisco: Jossey-Bass.

Schoonmaker, F. (1998). Promise and possibility: Learning to teach. *Teachers College Record, 99*(3), 559–591.

Schwab, J. J. (1970). *The practical: A language for curriculum*. Washington, DC: National Educational Association.

Shulman, L. S. (1986). Those who understand: Knowledge growth in teaching. *Educational Researcher, 15*(2), 4–14.

Shulman, L. S. (1999). Taking learning seriously. *Change, 31*(4), 10–17.

Skemp, R. R. (1989). *Mathematics in the primary school*. London: Routledge.

Southall, C., & King, D. (1979). Critical incidents in student teaching. *Teacher Educator, 15*(2), 34–36.

Sumara, D. J., & Luce-Kapler, R. (1996). (Un)becoming a teacher: Negotiating identities while learning to teach. *Canadian Journal of Education, 21*, 65–83.

Swanson, H. L., & O'Connor, J. E., & Cooney, J. B. (1990). An information processing analysis of expert and novice teachers' problem solving. *American Educational Research Journal, 27*(3), 533–556.

Townsend, R. G., & Robinson, N. (1994). Making the politics of education even more interesting. In J. Scribner & D. Layton (Eds.), *Studying the politics of education*. (pp. 185–199). New York: Falmer Press.

Weinstein, C. S. (1988). Preservice teachers' expectations about the first year of teaching. *Teaching & Teaching Education, 4*, 31–40.

Weinstein, C. S. (1989). Teacher education students' preconceptions of teaching. *Teaching and Teacher Education, 40*(2), 53–60.

Weinstein, C., Woolfolk, A. E., Dittmeier, L., Shanker, U. (1994). Protector or prison guard? Using metaphors and media to explore student teachers' thinking about classroom management. *Action in Teacher Education, 16,* 41–54.

Wilkins-Carter, E. A. (1997). The nature and effectiveness of feedback given by cooperating teachers to student teachers. *Teacher Educator, 32*(4), 235–249.

Wood, E., & Geddis, A. N. (1999). Self-conscious narrative and teacher education: Representing practice in professional course work. *Teaching and Teacher Education, 15*(1), 107–119.

Zeichner, K. M., & Gore, J.M. (1990). Teacher socilizaiton. In W.R. Houston (Ed.), *Handbook of research in teacher education* (pp. 329–348). New York: MacMillian.

Zeichner, K. M., & Liston, D. P. (1987). Teaching students to reflect. *Harvard Educational Review, 57*(1), 23–48.

INDEX